Our Children, Our Church

Child Protection
Policies and Procedures
for the
Catholic Church in Ireland

The Irish Bishops' Conference
The Conference of Religious of Ireland
The Irish Missionary Union

First published 2005 by
Veritas Publications
7/8 Lower Abbey Street
Dublin 1
Ireland
Email publications@veritas.ie
Website www.veritas.ie

ISBN 1 85390 918 1

Printed in the Republic of Ireland by Betaprint, Dublin

*Veritas books are printed on paper made from the wood pulp of managed forests. For
every tree felled, at least one tree is planted, thereby renewing natural resources.*

Contents

Acknowledgements   ix
Introduction   1

Part One
Principles and Structures   5

Chapter
One   **Guiding Principles**   6
      1.1   Introduction   6
      1.2   Principles from Gospel Values   6
      1.3   Principles from International Law   6
      1.4   Principles from Domestic Legislation   7
      1.5   Principles for the Church's Child Protection Policy   7
      1.6   Support for the Role of the Family   8
      1.7   A One-Church Policy   9
      1.8   Church Organisations and Existing Procedures   9
      1.9   Where the Church is, Children will be Safe   10

Two   **Structures**   11
      2.1   Introduction   11
      2.2   National Structures   11
      2.3   'Collaborative Units'   13
      2.4   Diocesan and Congregational Structures within the
              'Collaborative Units'   14
      2.5   Parish Structures   15
      2.6   Non-Parish Institutions   16
      2.7   Annual Audit   17
      2.8   Review and Evaluation   17

Part Two
Good Practice for the Safeguarding of Children   19

Three   **Best Practice in Working with Children
                   and Young People**   **20**
    3.1   Introduction   20
    3.2   Code of Good Practice for Church Organisations   20

Four   **Recruitment and Training of Employees
                   and Volunteers**   **28**
    4.1   Introduction   28
    4.2   Recruitment Process   28
    4.3   Induction and Training   30

Five   **Selection and Formation of Candidates for
                   the Priesthood and Religious Life**   **33**
    5.1   Introduction   33
    5.2   Selection of Candidates   33
    5.3   Formation   33
    5.4   Transfer from other Dioceses and Jurisdictions   35

Part Three
Responding to Allegations and Suspicions of Child Abuse 37

Six   **Key Elements of a Response**   **38**

6.1   Introduction   38
6.2   An Inter-Agency Approach   38
6.3   Exchange of Information   38
6.4   Referring Child Abuse to the Civil Authorities   38
6.5   Reasonable Grounds for Concern   39
6.6   Existing Procedures   39
6.7   Confidentiality   39
6.8   Prompt and Appropriate Response   40
6.9   Recording of Information   40

Seven   **Definition of Child Abuse**   **41**

7.1   Introduction   41
7.2   What is Child Abuse?   41
7.3   Forms of Child Abuse   41
7.4   Children with Special Vulnerabilities   43
7.5   Peer Abuse   43

Eight   **Initial Response and Reporting Procedures**   **44**

8.1   Introduction   44
8.2   Importance of Procedures   44
8.3   Supports and Structures within the Church   44
8.4   Encountering Allegations or Suspicions   45
8.5   The Church's Dual Responsibility   45
8.6   Procedures for Responding to Allegations of Child Abuse   46
8.7   Procedures for Responding to Suspicions of Child Abuse   48
8.8   Historical Allegations   50
8.9   Inappropriate Behaviour and Misconduct   51
8.10   Allegations or Suspicions not involving Church Personnel   51

Nine   **Post-Reporting Issues**   **52**
    9.1   Introduction   52
    9.2   Actions Following Reporting   52
    9.3   Next Stages in Procedures: Priests or Religious   53
    9.4   Next Stages in Procedures: Lay Employees or
          Volunteers   53

Ten   **Canon Law Procedures**   **55**
    10.1 Introduction   55
    10.2 Procedures Relating to Diocesan Priests
          and Religious Clergy   55
    10.3 Procedures Relating to Religious who are not
          Ordained   59
    10.4 Procedures Relating to a Bishop or Religious Superior 61
    10.5 Procedures where Child Abuse is Non-Sexual   61

Eleven   **Outcome of Civil Investigation**   **63**
    11.1 Investigation Process   63
    11.2 Outcome of Investigation   64

Twelve   **Protecting Against Future Risk**   **66**
    12.1 Introduction   66
    12.2 Assessment and Treatment   66
    12.3 Future Status Regarding Ministry   67
    12.4 Supervision   69

Thirteen **Promoting Healing and Reconciliation**   **71**
    13.1 Introduction   71
    13.2 Victims of Abuse and their Families   71
    13.3 Local Church Communities   73
    13.4 The Person Accused   75
    13.5 Family of the Person Accused   75
    13.6 Colleagues of the Person Accused   76

Appendices 79

One   Working Group on Child Protection   80

Two   Written Submissions to the Working Group
on Child Protection: Main Points   81

Three   Key Legislative Provisions   83

Four   Recommended Supervision Ratios   84

Five   Sample Application Form for
Volunteers   85

Six   Sample Declaration Form to be Completed by
Staff and Volunteers   87

Seven   Pre-Employment Consultancy Service
(Northern Ireland)   88

Eight   Sample Questionnaire for the Bishop or Religious Superior of a
Priest or Religious Applying for Transfer   89

Nine   Clearance for a Member of a Religious
Congregation Transferring to Ireland   92

Ten   Role of State Agencies   93

Eleven   Signs and Symptoms of Child Abuse   95

Endnotes   99

Acknowledgements

The Irish Bishops' Conference, The Conference of Religious of Ireland and The Irish Missionary Union (the Sponsoring Bodies) wish to express their gratitude to Ms Maureen Lynott, Chairperson, and to the other members of the Child Protection Working Group for their valuable contribution to the development of the guidelines contained in *Our Children, Our Church*.

The Sponsoring Bodies would also like to thank the many people who contributed in various ways to the work of the Group – including those who attended consultation meetings, the organisations and individuals who made written submissions, those who commented on successive drafts of the document, and the Child Protection Office and Committee of the Irish Bishops' Conference. Their input in preparing these guidelines is greatly appreciated.

Finally, thanks are extended to those who provided editorial expertise and administrative support in the preparation and publication of the document.

Introduction

Purpose of this Document

The purpose of this document is to provide a set of policies and procedures for those who have responsibility for the protection of children and young people in the life of the Catholic Church in Ireland.

The document expresses the commitment of the Church to best practice in this area, including the development of effective structures for safeguarding children, for responding to suspicions or allegations of child abuse and for providing pastoral supports and training.

Following the publication of *Child Sexual Abuse: Framework for a Church Response*[1] in 1996, each diocese and institute of religious life sought to implement the guidelines it provided and to develop them in accordance with its own particular circumstances.

This present document, *Our Children, Our Church*, provides a more comprehensive and unified approach to child protection across the Catholic Church in Ireland. In particular, by proposing a single national structure for the monitoring and managing of child protection issues, it aims to bring greater clarity and consistency to the Church's procedures in relation to child protection.

Whereas *Child Sexual Abuse: Framework for a Church Response* was concerned solely with child sexual abuse, the guidance in this document relates to all forms of abuse – physical, sexual and emotional abuse and neglect. The document also provides principles and procedures for a wider range of issues related to child protection. The guidance it provides is relevant to all who work in Church-based institutions or organisations, in any capacity.

In recent years, the statutory authorities, in both legal jurisdictions in Ireland, have published comprehensive civil guidelines in relation to child protection.[2] The guidance contained in this document is based on these official guidelines.

Our Children, Our Church also reflects the recommendations of research commissioned by the Irish Bishops' Conference from the Health Research Centre, Department of Psychology, Royal College of Surgeons in Ireland, and published as *Time to Listen: Confronting Child Sexual Abuse by Catholic Clergy in Ireland*.[3]

Child Protection Working Group

A key element in developing the guidance contained in *Our Children, Our Church* was the advice and expertise of the Child Protection Working Group established in June 2003 by the three Sponsoring Bodies: The Irish Bishops' Conference, The Conference of Religious of Ireland and The Irish Missionary Union. The Working Group, chaired by Maureen Lynott, was commissioned with the task of developing a child protection policy for the Catholic Church in Ireland.[4]

The terms of reference of the Child Protection Working Group were:

> To develop a comprehensive and integrated child protection policy for the Irish Catholic Church. This policy will encompass all Church-related activities and personnel (including volunteers) in Ireland, North and South. The policy will be rooted in best practice for the safety and welfare of children, and specific guidance on the management of concerns and allegations regarding child protection. The policy will be consistent with civil law, *Children First, Co-operating to Safeguard Children* and relevant statutory procedures. It will also be consistent with all relevant Church Law so as to be normative.

Method and Process of the Working Group

In carrying out its task, the Working Group engaged in a process of listening, consultation, obtaining the advice of experts, reflection and discussion. It considered previous Church policies such as *Child Sexual Abuse: Framework for a Church Response* and the policies of the Catholic Church in other jurisdictions, notably England and Wales, Scotland, the USA and Australia.

Consultation with children and young people

The Working Group consulted with some children and young people to hear about their experiences and their views concerning involvement in the Church, and their suggestions as to how their involvement and participation could be increased.

Key themes that emerged in the listening sessions with children and young people were their strong desire to actively participate in Church life (even though current participation rates are low and activities for children and young people limited); their interest in and identification with the Church of their baptism; their wish to be consulted more about their faith and Church matters relevant to them; their wish to be listened to; their desire to be invited to participate in the activities of the Church.

Consultation with adults who suffered child abuse by Church personnel

The Working Group also listened to representatives of adult groups who had experienced child abuse within the Church. Some of the key points raised were: the need for the Church to listen; the need for training; the need for consistent implementation and monitoring of child protection practices, and clear accountability and leadership; the responsibility of colleagues and other professionals to report child abuse; the need for a process of reconciliation and healing.

The Working Group members reported that the pain which many of those interviewed had experienced, and continue to experience, was palpable at some of the meetings. They also reported that one of the greatest losses felt by some of those who had been abused was their loss of faith, which in some cases had affected subsequent generations of their family. Others spoke of the shattering of their sense of trust in the Church. It was clear that some of those who were abused continue to seek reconciliation with the Church, while all continue to want a sense of closure.

Consultation with clergy and religious

Consultation sessions were held in Belfast, Dublin, Galway, Maynooth and Cork, and included bishops, religious superiors, diocesan priests, members of religious congregations and others working within the Church. The themes which arose most consistently were: the need to see child protection as a 'one-Church' responsibility; the need for consistent implementation of the new policies and procedures; recognition of the pastoral needs of all those affected by child abuse; concerns about the issue of 'stepping aside' and administrative leave; fear of false allegations; balancing the paramountcy of the child's needs with natural justice for the accused person; the need for support and training in relation to child protection.

Consultation with parents

During consultative meetings, parents expressed feelings of distance from the Church but also their strong desire for the Church to move forward in an open and accountable way regarding child welfare and protection. They spoke about the lack of communication with regard to the positive steps that have been taken by the Church in relation to safeguarding children; the lack of information, as well as the lack of prompt, effective and sensitive communication by the Church with those affected by abuse.

Written submissions

The Working Group invited written submissions from a large number of statutory and voluntary organisations. It also advertised in the main national newspapers of the Republic of Ireland and Northern Ireland. A total of 113 submissions were received from the general public, the voluntary sector, organisations representing children and young people, religious organisations and statutory agencies, including some health boards, social services trusts and government departments.[5]

Completion of the process

Having drawn together all these responses, and following discussion and analysis, the members of the Working Group prepared a series of drafts of the proposed comprehensive and integrated child protection policy for the Church. In the latter stages of this process, the Sponsoring Bodies, through their representatives on the Steering Committee, worked with Maureen Lynott to resolve outstanding issues.

PART ONE

Principles and Structures

There are two chapters in Part One of *Our Children, Our Church.*

Chapter One sets out the principles, derived from both Gospel values and civil guidelines, which inform the Church's policies and procedures for protecting children and for responding appropriately to allegations and suspicions of child abuse.

Chapter Two outlines the structures to be established to ensure effective and consistent implementation of the procedures throughout the whole Church and in all parts of the country.

1 Guiding Principles

1.1 Introduction

All children have a fundamental right to be respected, nurtured, cared for and protected. This right is embedded in Gospel values, in international law and in domestic law.

The rights of the child

> ... exist because children are human beings with intrinsic dignity and irreducible worth. They do not ask to be born, and justice and freedom are therefore their birthright. For children 'freedom' includes the possibility to grow and develop free from neglect, harm, abuse and exploitation ... 'Justice' includes access to basic care and nurture in a safe, permanent, stable environment. This includes freedom from the injustices of abuse, neglect, and exploitation.[6]

1.2 Principles from Gospel Values[7]

Children occupy a central place in the teachings of Jesus, who pointed to the child as the ultimate symbol of the kingdom of God. 'Whoever does not receive the kingdom of God like a child shall not enter it' (Lk 18:17). This places a sacred obligation on the Church, called to bear witness to the presence of the kingdom in the world, to ensure that children are welcomed, cherished and protected in a manner consistent with their central place in the life of the Church. The fact that Jesus reserved some of his severest warnings for those who would knowingly undermine the faith of one of these 'little ones' is a solemn reminder of the collective obligation of the Church to ensure the care and protection of children and young people.

1.3 Principles from International Law

The Preamble to the United Nations Convention on the Rights of the Child, to which Ireland, the United Kingdom and the Holy See are signatories, states that the child is entitled to be brought up 'in the spirit of peace, dignity, tolerance, freedom, equality and solidarity'. The Preamble recalls that the Universal Declaration of Human Rights proclaimed that 'childhood is entitled to special care and assistance'. In specific articles, the Convention states the principle that 'in all actions concerning children ... the best interests of the child shall be a primary consideration'; the right of the child to be protected from all forms of sexual exploitation and sexual abuse and from any other kind of exploitation or abuse; the obligation of States Parties to take all appropriate measures to promote the physical and psychological recovery and social re-integration of children who have been the victims of abuse or exploitation.[8]

1.4 Principles from Domestic Legislation

In both jurisdictions in Ireland, legislation on child welfare, and civil guidelines for child protection,[9] accord central importance to the principle that the welfare of the child should be the first and paramount consideration. This means that in all decisions made and actions taken in response to suspicions or allegations of child abuse, 'the child's welfare must always be paramount and this overrides all other considerations'.[10]

1.5 Principles for the Church's Child Protection Policy

The policies and procedures outlined in *Our Children, Our Church* are guided by principles derived from both Gospel values and civil sources, including the principle that the welfare of the child is the first and paramount consideration.

The principles derived from Gospel values are:

- Each child shall be cherished and affirmed as a gift from God with an inherent right to dignity of life and bodily integrity which shall be respected, nurtured and protected by all.
- Everyone in the Church has an obligation to ensure that the fundamental rights of children are respected.
- A child's right to safety and care is inalienable.
- Children have a right to an environment free from abuse or neglect.
- Children have a fundamental right to justice and freedom; they have a right to be listened to and to be heard.
- Children have a right to good role models whom they can fully trust, who will respect them and nurture their spiritual, physical and emotional development.
- Those who have suffered child abuse by Church personnel should receive a compassionate and just response and should be offered appropriate pastoral care as they seek to rebuild their lives.

The principles derived from civil sources are:

- All adults have a duty to report allegations or suspicions of child abuse, where reasonable grounds for concern exist, irrespective of the status of the person suspected or their relationship to them or to the child.
- Due regard must be given to the criminal dimension of any action.
- It is the statutory duty of the civil authorities, not individuals or organisations, to investigate reports of child abuse.
- A proper balance must be maintained between protecting children and respecting the needs and rights of carers and adults; however, where there is a conflict, the welfare of the child must be paramount.
- Actions taken to protect a child should not in themselves be abusive or cause the child unnecessary distress. Every action and procedure should consider the overall needs of the child.
- Organisations have a corporate responsibility to operate effective systems to assure the protection of children. They should ensure best practice in relation to recruitment and selection processes, provide appropriate training and ensure that all personnel are aware of their responsibility both to prevent child abuse and to report concerns about child abuse.
- All agencies and disciplines concerned with the protection and welfare of children must work cooperatively in the best interests of children.

1.6 Support for the Role of the Family

Parents have primary responsibility for ensuring the education, protection and development of their children. The family is the place where children learn to value themselves and others, to trust and to love.

A fundamental principle of *Our Children, Our Church* is that all personnel working for the Church should act in support of parents and guardians in the exercise of their responsibility for the care and formation of their children. This includes providing parents and guardians with information about all aspects of their child's engagement in the life of the Church.

1.7   A One-Church Policy

This document sets out a one-Church approach to child protection. It aims to ensure that the same principles and procedures for safeguarding children and for responding to allegations or suspicions of child abuse operate at every level and in every place throughout the Church in Ireland.

The care and protection of children is the responsibility of the whole Church and is a requirement that applies regardless of the nature of the Church activities in which children are involved. Everyone who participates in the life of the Church has a role to play in creating an environment in which children can develop and be safe.

A further aim of the one-Church policy is to create a secure and supportive atmosphere in which those who have suffered abuse can disclose this to a trusted person in the expectation of a sensitive, caring and compassionate response.

Support for the implementation of the procedures in *Our Children, Our Church* will be offered to all Church organisations and personnel through the structures outlined in Chapter Two. It is the responsibility of every organisation within the Church and of all Church personnel to ensure that the procedures are applied in their own sphere of activity.

It is also the responsibility of Church organisations to ensure that the principles and procedures contained in this document are widely publicised. Experience shows that awareness and understanding are critical to ensuring the effective implementation of child protection policies and procedures.

In particular, the accessibility of information is of central importance in providing an appropriate response when concerns about child protection arise. Key information to enable people to act on child protection concerns should be available in parishes and all other Church-sponsored organisations, and should be publicly displayed on notice boards in church entrances, in youth clubs and other relevant places.

1.8   Church Organisations and Existing Procedures

Many Church organisations come under the direct responsibility of government departments which already have procedures for reporting allegations and suspicions of child abuse. Where such procedures exist, *they* should be followed rather than the procedures outlined in Chapter Eight of this document.

1.9 Where the Church is, Children will be Safe

In the light of the principles from civil policy and the teaching of the Church which inform this document, the leadership of the Catholic Church in Ireland undertakes to do all in its power to ensure that where the Church is, children will be safe.

The leadership of the Catholic Church is committed to taking the necessary steps to:

- Cherish and safeguard children and young people.
- Foster best practice.
- Ensure accountability through establishing effective structures.
- Support Church organisations and personnel in safeguarding children.
- Respond effectively to allegations and suspicions of child abuse within the Church and to cooperate with the civil authorities.
- Take just and appropriate action in relation to Church personnel who have abused children and to take effective measures against future risk to children.
- Promote healing and reconciliation.

2.1 Introduction

The establishment of appropriate structures is required to maximise the effectiveness of child protection procedures throughout the Church in Ireland. The proposed structures reflect the importance of dioceses and religious congregations working in collaboration with one another. The structures are informed by the key principles outlined in Chapter One, which include a commitment to a single set of policies and procedures for safeguarding children and for responding to complaints of child abuse, and a commitment to providing support and training for those who deal with child protection issues.

2.2 National Structures

2.2.1 National Board for Child Protection

The Sponsoring Bodies will establish a National Board for Child Protection. This Board will include professionals from child care, psychology, theology, law, academia, education and business, and will include parents.

It will be separate from any other secretariat or office of the Irish Bishops' Conference or religious congregations and will have overall responsibility for ensuring that the Church's policies and procedures for child protection are implemented, monitored and publicised.

Its specific functions will be to:

- Oversee the implementation of the policies and procedures contained in *Our Children, Our Church*.
- Liaise regularly with the civil agencies responsible for child protection with a view to ensuring awareness of developments in legislation, policy and practice.
- Advise the Sponsoring Bodies on best practice in relation to child protection policies and procedures.
- Establish a Professional Practice Committee.
- Give professional advice and moral support to the 'Collaborative Units' (Section 2.3) and to other Church organisations.
- Support the 'Collaborative Units' in developing appropriate training strategies.
- Serve as a national training resource for Church personnel.

- Maintain a central and confidential database of all cases of child abuse involving Church personnel.
- Maintain and publish national statistics in relation to child abuse involving Church personnel.
- Liaise at a central level with the civil authorities, professional bodies, other churches and other national offices for child protection.
- Review and audit the implementation of the policies and procedures of *Our Children, Our Church* in each 'Collaborative Unit'.
- Publish an annual report on the implementation of the policies and procedures contained in *Our Children, Our Church*.

National Office for Child Protection

The National Board for Child Protection shall establish a National Office for Child Protection to implement its policies and decisions.

Chief Executive

The National Board will recruit and appoint a Chief Executive and other personnel, with the agreement of the Sponsoring Bodies, to enable the Board to discharge its functions.

2.2.2 Professional Practice Committee

The National Board for Child Protection shall convene a national resource to be known as the Professional Practice Committee. The function of this Committee will be to advise and support bishops and religious superiors in deciding the future of Church personnel where there has been a conviction for child abuse, or where such abuse has been admitted or established, but there has not been a conviction. The membership of this Committee will comprise experts in child care and child protection, law, psychiatry, psychology and canon law.

Where complainants or accused persons, or both, are dissatisfied with the response of the relevant Church authority to a complaint of child abuse, the option of a review of the procedures undertaken should be available to either party. The review will be an independent evaluation of whether the principles and procedures of the Church as outlined in this document have been observed. A review of whether procedures have been adhered to in a particular case does not entail a review of its actual outcome, unless the Church authority requests the reviewer to consider this aspect. The Professional Practice Committee will appoint the reviewer.

2.3 'Collaborative Units'

2.3.1 Process for establishing 'Collaborative Units'

One of the first tasks of the National Board for Child Protection will be to consider, in consultation with the Sponsoring Bodies, the development of 'Collaborative Units'.

The purpose of these 'Units' will be to ensure that every bishop and religious superior has available to them the necessary advice, support and expertise in relation to child protection issues.

Each 'Collaborative Unit' will ensure that an effective response to allegations and suspicions of child abuse is in place in each diocese and religious congregation within its area of responsibility. Each 'Unit' will have assigned to it a Director of Child Protection to provide professional case management and ensure consistency of practice.

'Collaborative Units' will also ensure ongoing collaboration between bishops and religious superiors in child protection matters, the provision of necessary resources, and effective training and pastoral responses.

The number of 'Collaborative Units' shall be determined by the National Board for Child Protection, in consultation with the Sponsoring Bodies. The decision on the number of Units and the areas they will cover will be guided by an assessment of the needs of each diocese and religious congregation, the desire to ensure that each diocese and religious congregation is part of an appropriate 'Collaborative Unit', and by the need to concentrate the professional expertise required to implement the Church's procedures on child protection.

2.3.2 Child Protection Management Group

Each 'Collaborative Unit' shall have a Child Protection Management Group whose expertise will be available to individual dioceses and congregations within that Unit. The chairperson and members of the Group will be appointed jointly by the relevant bishops and religious superiors. The Group should include child care professionals, a lawyer, a communications officer, a parent representative, an education or youth ministry professional, a canon lawyer, a priest and a religious. Other experts may be called on by the Director of Child Protection as the need arises.

The Child Protection Management Group should meet at least quarterly to monitor the overall response to allegations and suspicions of child abuse within the 'Collaborative Unit', including the appropriate implementation of pastoral care arrangements.

2.3.3 Director of Child Protection

In each 'Collaborative Unit', the relevant bishops and religious superiors shall, with the advice and support of the Child Protection Management Group, appoint a professionally qualified Director of Child Protection to discharge the following functions:

- Receive referrals of allegations and suspicions of child abuse.
- Liaise closely with the bishops or religious superiors regarding specific cases.
- Liaise with the civil authorities and ensure that they are involved with appropriate speed.
- Take account of the immediate danger to children and recommend appropriate action.
- Provide professional expertise and support in regard to decision-making in individual cases.
- Ensure appropriate steps are taken in relation to an accused person while enquiries are under way.
- Provide support in relation to the delivery of training.
- Provide support in the delivery of pastoral care.
- Support dioceses and congregations in the discharge of their responsibilities in regard to child protection.
- Liaise effectively with and provide information to the National Office for Child Protection on all issues related to child protection.

Where there is a difference of opinion between the bishop or religious superior and the Director of Child Protection in relation to any recommendation or action to be taken in the implementation of the procedures outlined in this document, this shall be recorded in writing and signed by both parties. Either party can request that the matter be reviewed by the National Board for Child Protection.

2.4 Diocesan and Congregational Structures within the 'Collaborative Units'

2.4.1 Diocesan or congregational Child Protection Committee

In consultation with the National Board, each bishop and religious superior shall appoint a Child Protection Committee as a resource both for themselves and for their diocese or religious congregation. Smaller religious congregations and dioceses may, where appropriate, jointly appoint a Child Protection Committee or a religious congregation may request a diocesan Child Protection Committee to act on its behalf.

The Child Protection Committee shall include among its membership relevant experts, parish representatives and representatives from appropriate agencies. The Committee shall have responsibility for:

- Ensuring that the diocese or religious congregation implements the guidelines contained in this document and in civil procedures.
- Ensuring that information about child protection is readily accessible in parishes and Church organisations.
- Ensuring that referrals are made promptly to the Director of Child Protection following complaints of child abuse.
- Ensuring that appropriate pastoral care is provided to complainants and their families, to accused persons and their families and colleagues, and to parishes.
- Ensuring the planning and delivery of training in child protection for all Church personnel in the diocese or religious congregation.
- Liaising with the National Office for Child Protection on arrangements and procedures.
- Publishing an annual report outlining developments in regard to each element of the Committee's responsibilities.

2.4.2 Diocesan or congregational Child Protection Coordinator

Each bishop and religious superior will appoint a Child Protection Coordinator. This appointment will be made with the support and advice of the Child Protection Committee, which will oversee the work of the Coordinator.

The Child Protection Coordinator should have the personal qualities, interest and life experience that would fit him or her to undertake the tasks involved. The Coordinator need not be professionally qualified or be employed full-time on child protection matters. However, in some of the larger dioceses and religious congregations, employment of a Coordinator on a full-time basis may be necessary.

He or she will be given a role specification, be required to undergo training and will also be able to draw on expert help and support from the Director of Child Protection.

2.5 Parish Structures

2.5.1 Commitment at parish level

Children's involvement in Church activities takes place mainly at parish level. It is at this level, therefore, that the need for awareness of principles and procedures for child protection is greatest and where the commitment of everyone involved with children is crucial.

2.5.2 Parish Child Protection Representative

In each parish, a Parish Child Protection Representative will be appointed. In the case of small parishes, a clustering arrangement with a neighbouring parish or parishes may be considered.

The responsibilities of the Parish Child Protection Representative will be:

- To promote awareness of the Church's child protection policies, as outlined in this document.
- To ensure that the public has ready access to contact details for the Director of Child Protection.
- To facilitate anyone in the parish in bringing an allegation or suspicion of child abuse to the attention of the Director of Child Protection, should they wish to have such support.
- The Parish Child Protection Representative should be appointed by the parish after appropriate consultation and agreement with the diocese. The person appointed should have the personal qualities, interest and life experience fitting to the tasks involved. The Representative need not be a paid employee, nor a professional or expert and is likely to be a lay person. He or she will be given a role specification, be required to undergo training and will be able to draw on expert help and support from the Director of Child Protection.

2.5.3 Making information available

To assist the reporting of child protection concerns, the contact details of the relevant Director of Child Protection will be made widely available at parish level. They will, for example, be displayed in clearly visible and accessible places, such as the entrance to churches and in other relevant community buildings. The contact details for the Parish Child Protection Representative will also be readily accessible.

2.6 Non-Parish Institutions

All Catholic-run institutions[11] should have similar policies, procedures and arrangements to those in parishes and should therefore have a designated Child Protection Representative.

2.7 Annual Audit

The National Board for Child Protection will conduct an annual audit of the implementation of the policies and procedures contained in this document, including the response of the Church nationally and of each 'Collaborative Unit' to allegations and suspicions of child abuse.

Protocols for this process will be established by the National Board for Child Protection; these will include an opportunity for both the Sponsoring Bodies and the 'Collaborative Units' to indicate, in advance of the publication of the audit, their proposed plan of action in response to its findings.

2.8 Review and Evaluation

The operation of the policies, procedures and implementation structures outlined in *Our Children, Our Church* shall be reviewed and evaluated after a period of three years from the establishment of the National Board for Child Protection.

PART TWO

Good Practice for the Safeguarding of Children

Part Two of *Our Children, Our Church* covers good practice for ensuring the safety and well-being of children and young people during their participation in the life of the Church and in the activities of Church-related organisations.

Chapter Three describes the key elements of good practice for child protection which should be applied by all Church institutions and organisations working with children and young people.

Chapter Four outlines good practice procedures for the recruitment, training and management of employees and volunteers.

Chapter Five deals with the selection and formation of candidates for the priesthood and religious life. It deals also with requirements regarding child protection which arise in the context of the transfer of a priest or religious from one diocese or religious congregation to another.

3 Best Practice in Working with Children and Young People

3.1 Introduction

The participation of children and young people in the Church spans a wide range of activities and levels of engagement with Church personnel, including involvement in the celebration of the sacraments, altar serving, choirs, membership of youth clubs, play groups and sports activities.

To enhance and encourage the participation of children and young people in Church life and activities, it is important that they can feel that their contribution will enrich the Church and that their voices will be heard and valued. It is also important to reassure them that their safety and well-being are paramount considerations at all times.

Likewise, it is essential to reassure parents and guardians that all steps have been taken to ensure best practice in relation to the care of their children. Their confidence in the safety of Church activities is of critical importance. Consultation with and involvement of parents and guardians and families is a necessary ingredient in the engagement of children and young people in Church activities.

This chapter gives general guidance on good practice for ensuring a safe environment for children and young people.[12] Any group operating in a Church setting, including visiting groups, should be made aware of the policies and procedures for child protection in operation in the organisation or parish and should be asked to confirm that it will implement these policies and procedures.

3.2 Code of Good Practice for Church Organisations

Children and young people need warmth and security in order to thrive. Fostering a nurturing and affirming environment is therefore an essential element of Church activities. This should always be reflected in the practice of those who work with children and young people.

A customised Code of Good Practice for working with children should be drawn up by all organisations or groups within the Church. The aim of this is to ensure the safety of children and young people, to enhance the work practices of Church personnel, and to reassure parents and guardians, as well as children themselves, that there is a commitment to best practice.

The Code should recognise the imbalance in power inherent in adult–child relationships. It should include positive child-centred statements about the importance of:

- listening to children and young people;
- valuing and respecting them as individuals;
- rewarding their efforts as well as achievements;
- involving them in decision making (where appropriate);
- encouraging and praising them.

Each group or organisation should designate a Child Protection Representative and should make known to personnel, and to children and parents, who this person is. The Child Protection Representative will have initial responsibility for dealing with matters relating to child welfare and protection (Chapter Two, Section 2.5.2).

3.2.1 Code of Behaviour for Church personnel

The Code of Behaviour for Church personnel working with children which is outlined below is a general guide. Although it may need to be adapted for particular situations, its key principles should be adhered to as far as possible.

The Code of Behaviour adopted by a Church organisation should be read, understood and signed by all personnel, including volunteers, on joining or participating in the activities of the group. The Code should include a disciplinary procedure to be used in the event of a worker or volunteer breaching any of its requirements. It should also include a complaints procedure.

The key issues that should be covered in a Code of Behaviour for workers in Church organisations are as follows:

General conduct
- Physical punishment of children is not permissible under any circumstances.
- Verbal abuse of children or telling jokes of a sexual nature in the presence of children can never be acceptable. Great care should be taken if it is necessary to have a conversation regarding sexual matters with a child or young person.
- Being alone with a child or young person may not always be wise or appropriate practice. If a situation arises where it is necessary to be alone with a child, another responsible adult should be informed immediately, by telephone if necessary. A diary note that the meeting with the young person took place, including the reasons for it, should be made.
- Best practice in relation to travel with children and young people should be observed. Personnel should not undertake any car or

minibus journey alone with a child or young person. If, in certain circumstances, only one adult is available, there should be a minimum of two children or young people present for the entire journey. In the event of an emergency, where it is necessary to make a journey alone with a child, a record of this should be made and the child's parent or guardian should be informed as soon as possible.

- Children and young people should not be permitted to work or remain in churches, parish property or schools unless there are at least two adults present.
- All children and young people must be treated with equal respect; favouritism is not acceptable.
- Personnel should not engage in or tolerate any behaviour – verbal, psychological or physical – that could be construed as bullying or abusive.
- A disproportionate amount of time should not be spent with any particular child or group of children.
- Under no circumstances should Church personnel give alcohol, tobacco or drugs to children or young people.
- Alcohol, tobacco or drugs must not be used by personnel who are supervising or working with children and young people.
- Only age-appropriate language, material on media products (such as camera phones, internet, video) and activities should be used when working with children and young people. Sexually explicit or pornographic material is never acceptable.

Respect for physical integrity
- The physical integrity of children and young people must be respected at all times.
- Personnel must not engage in inappropriate physical contact of any kind – including tough physical play, physical reprimand and horseplay (tickling, wrestling). This should not prevent appropriate contact in situations where it is necessary to ensure the safety and well-being of a child (for example, where a child is distressed).

Respect for privacy
- The right to privacy of children and young people must be respected at all times.
- Particular care regarding privacy must be taken when young people are in locations such as changing areas, swimming pools, showers and toilets.

- Photographs of children or young people must never be taken while they are in changing areas (for example, in a locker room or bathing facility).
- Tasks of a personal nature (for example, helping with toileting, washing or changing clothing) should not be done for children or young people if they can undertake these tasks themselves.

Meetings with children and young people
- If the pastoral care of a child or young person necessitates meeting alone with them, such meetings should not be held in an isolated environment. The times and designated locations for meetings should allow for transparency and accountability (for example, be held in rooms with a clear glass panel or window, in buildings where other people are present, and with the door of the room left open).
- Both the length and number of meetings should be limited.
- Parents or guardians should be informed that the meeting(s) took place, except in circumstances where to do so might place the child in danger.
- Visits to the home or private living quarters of Church personnel should not be encouraged, nor should meetings be conducted in such locations.
- When the need for a visit to the home of a child or young person arises, professional boundaries must be observed at all times.

Children with special needs or disability
- Children with special needs or disability may depend on adults more than other children for their care and safety, and so sensitivity and clear communication are particularly important.
- Where it is necessary to carry out tasks of a personal nature for a child with special needs, this should be done with the full understanding and consent of parents or guardians.
- In carrying out such personal care tasks, sensitivity must be shown to the child and the tasks should be undertaken with the utmost discretion.
- Any care task of a personal nature which a child or young person can do for themselves should not be undertaken by a worker.
- In an emergency situation where this type of help is required, parents should be fully informed as soon as is reasonably possible.

Vulnerable children
- Since especially vulnerable children may depend on adults more

than other children for their care and safety, sensitivity and clear communication are of utmost importance.

- Workers should be aware that vulnerable children may be more likely than other children to be bullied or subjected to other forms of abuse, and may also be less clear about physical and emotional boundaries.
- It is particularly important that vulnerable children should be carefully listened to, in recognition of the fact that they may have difficulty in expressing their concerns and in order that the importance of what they say is not underestimated.

3.2.2 Code of Behaviour for Children
Developing a code of behaviour
Children and young people feel more secure when they know the limits of and boundaries appropriate to their own behaviour and that of others. In recognition of this, and in order to create an environment in which children feel valued, encouraged and affirmed, it is important to develop an appropriate Code of Behaviour for Children. To maximise the sense of ownership of a Code of Behaviour, it is recommended that children and young people be consulted and included in the development of the Code for their own particular group. Age-appropriate language should be used as it is essential that children and young people can understand what is and what is not acceptable with regard to their behaviour and that of others.

Key elements
- The Code of Behaviour should reflect the dignity and rights of each child and should encourage respectful behaviour.
- The issue of appropriate response to breaches of discipline and to disruptive behaviour, including bullying, should be covered in the Code.
- The Code should make clear that discipline problems will be handled in partnership with parents and guardians.
- The Code should make reference to the organisation's complaints procedure and how to use it.

Implementing the code
- A copy of the Code should be given to all children and young people participating in activities, and to their parents or guardians.
- The Code should be clearly explained to each child or young person and should be signed by them (where appropriate).
- All staff and volunteers should be fully conversant with the Code of Behaviour for Children and its application.

3.2.3 Parental consent

- Church organisations should ensure that signed consent from parents or guardians is obtained prior to the participation of children and young people in events, activities and groups.
- Parents or guardians should be asked to indicate if their children have any specific dietary requirements, medical needs or special needs.

3.2.4 Record keeping

- An accurate record should be kept for each child and young person participating in activities, including, but not limited to, attendance, programme details and medical information.[13] This record should include a copy of the consent form or letter signed by the parent or guardian. It should also contain details of emergency contact numbers.
- A written record of organisers, supervisors, employees and volunteers in attendance at events, such as meetings, choir rehearsals and sports activities, should be kept.
- An Incident Report Form should be completed in the event of an accident or incident relating to a child.

3.2.5 Complaints procedure

- Organisations should develop a clear complaints procedure for use by young people or by parents who are dissatisfied with any aspect of activities or services provided.
- Children and young people and their parents or guardians should be given a copy of the complaints procedure and should be made aware of the procedure for making a complaint.
- All staff and volunteers should be informed about the complaints procedure.

3.2.6 Disruptive behaviour

- Should a child or young person display challenging or disruptive behaviour, it should be dealt with by more than one worker.
- A record should be made describing what happened, the circumstances of the incident, who was involved, whether any injury was sustained, or property damaged, and how the situation was resolved.
- In particular situations, further measures may need to be taken and parents or guardians may need to be involved.

3.2.7 Health and safety

- Adequate and appropriate supervision must be provided for all events and activities organised for children and young people (see Appendix Four for recommended ratios).
- Arrangements and procedures for leaving activities or centres should be explicit.
- In places such as changing areas, toilets and showers, separate provision should be made for boys and girls.
- There should be adequate and gender-appropriate supervision of boys and girls in such areas.
- A clear policy should be agreed with parents and guardians on the taking of photographs and the making of video recordings of children or young people involved in Church-related activities or events. This should also cover the generation of computer images. In addition, the policy should address the question of where and for what purpose photographs and images may be displayed.
- There should be regular health and safety reviews of facilities, procedures and practices.

3.2.8 Use of computers

Every Church organisation should have a clear policy in place regarding the use of email and the internet:

- Where a computer is used by more than one person, each person should be obliged to have a unique username and password, or where this is not possible, to maintain a signed record of the date, time and duration of their use of the computer.
- Where a computer in a Church organisation or institution can be accessed by children or young people, it should be accessible only through the use of a username and password unique to each child. Where this is not possible, the children or young people should be obliged to provide a signed record of the date, time and duration of their use of the computer.
- Computers which can be accessed by children or young people should always have appropriate filtering software.
- All computers in Church organisations and institutions should be monitored regularly to ensure that they are being used in accordance with the stated policy. Where there is any suspicion or doubt, a person with specialist knowledge of computer hardware and software should be asked to assess the purposes for which the computer has been used.

3.2.9 Trips away from home

- All trips, including day trips, overnight stays and holidays, need careful advance planning, including adequate provision for safety in regard to transport, facilities, activities and emergencies. Adequate insurance should be in place.
- Written consent by a parent or guardian specifically for each trip and related activities must be obtained well in advance.
- A copy of the itinerary and contact telephone numbers should be made available to parents and guardians.
- There must be adequate, gender-appropriate, supervision for boys and girls.
- Arrangements and procedures must be put in place to ensure that rules and appropriate boundaries are maintained in the relaxed environment of trips away.
- Particular attention should be given to ensuring that the privacy of young people is respected when they are away on trips.
- The provision of appropriate and adequate sleeping arrangements should be ensured in advance of the trip.
- Sleeping areas for boys and girls should be separate and supervised by two adults of the same sex as the group being supervised.
- At least two adults should be present in dormitories in which children or young people are sleeping. Under no circumstances should an adult share a bedroom with a young person.
- If, in an emergency situation, an adult considers it necessary to be in a children's dormitory or bedroom without another adult being present they should (a) immediately inform another adult in a position of responsibility and (b) make a diary note of the circumstances.

3.2.10 Pilgrimages and retreats

Pilgrimages and retreats are an important part of the Church's pastoral and spiritual engagement with children and young people. Those involved in the planning and delivery of pilgrimages and retreats should adhere to the same guidance as outlined for other activities with children and young people within the Church.

4 Recruitment and Training of Employees and Volunteers

4.1 Introduction

This chapter deals with those policies and procedures in regard to recruitment, training and management of Church employees and volunteers which help to protect children and young people and which develop the knowledge, skills and understanding of those entrusted to care for them.

4.2 Recruitment Process

4.2.1 General principles

'Safe practice starts with safe recruitment procedures.'[14] Most people who apply to work with children and young people in the Church are well-motivated and potentially suitable for the various tasks involved. It is most important, however, that all reasonable steps are taken to ensure that this is, in fact, the case. As well as enhancing the prospects of identifying the best person for the post, rigorous recruitment procedures can act as a deterrent to unsuitable applicants.

Some of the principles which enhance the safety of recruitment include:

- Always applying thorough selection procedures regardless of who the applicant is and whether the position is full-time, part-time, permanent, temporary, paid or voluntary.
- Judging the suitability of applicants across a broad range of criteria, through interview.
- Ensuring that interviews are conducted by more than one person and that at least one of those interviewing has established competence in interviewing and selection for posts involving work with children.
- Taking all reasonable steps to exclude unsuitable candidates by insisting on and verifying references, qualifications and previous records of employment.

4.2.2 Key issues in recruitment processes

The safety of recruitment processes can also be enhanced by ensuring that due attention is paid to the key issues outlined below.

Clear definition of role

A clear definition of role includes being specific about the roles and responsibilities that the person will be required to undertake, and identifying the personal qualities and skills needed to carry out the work. A detailed job description and information about the organisation or group responsible for the post should be sent to all applicants.

Written application

Applicants should be asked to supply information in writing. If an application form is used, it should be designed to collect all relevant information about the applicant, including past and current experience of working with children.[15] The information supplied by the applicant should be seen only by those directly involved in the recruitment process.

Interviews

Interviews should always be conducted by more than one representative of the group or organisation. The interview is a critical opportunity to explore with candidates the information provided in their written application and to assess their attitudes and skills, in particular their commitment to the welfare and protection of children.

The recommendation for appointment agreed by the interview panel should be submitted for ratification to the management committee of the organisation or group making the appointment.

Declarations

All applicants should be required to sign a declaration stating that there is no reason why they would be considered unsuitable to work with children or young people and declaring any past criminal convictions or cases pending.[16]

References

An applicant should be expected to supply the names of two referees, who are not family members, who will testify to their general character, their suitability for working with children and young people, and any other detail relevant to their ability to perform the tasks associated with the post. At least one referee should have first-hand knowledge of the applicant's previous work with children or young people.

An acceptable reference will indicate that the person is known to the referee and is considered by them to be suitable to work with children and young people. All references should be provided in writing and later verified by telephone, or in person.

References should be kept on file as part of the record of the recruitment process.

4.2.3 Vetting procedures

Once a person has been selected, and before they take up their appointment, the vetting procedures in the relevant jurisdiction should be utilised. This applies whether the person is clerical, religious, full-time or part-time, a lay employee or a volunteer.

In the Republic of Ireland, Garda vetting has been available only to the health authorities and some other designated agencies. However, following the expansion of the Garda Central Vetting Unit, vetting will be made available from early 2006 to all organisations employing staff to work with children and young people. Later, vetting will be extended to include volunteers.[17]

In Northern Ireland, personnel who have 'substantial access' to children, regardless of whether they are paid or not, should, where possible, be checked by the Pre-Employment Consultancy Service (PECS) prior to taking up work with children or young people.[18]

4.2.4 Records

Details of the selection and induction processes should be recorded and placed in the personnel file of the person appointed along with notes made during any part of the selection process, the application form, references and any other associated documentation.

A written record must be kept of the assessments made for each applicant for at least one year after they have been sent a letter stating that their application was unsuccessful. This is necessary because an unsuccessful applicant may bring a claim alleging discrimination in the selection process. Such a claim can be brought 'for up to six months after the date of the alleged act of discrimination, and an extension of six months is allowed where a good cause for not referring the claim within six months is established.'[19]

4.3 Induction and Training

4.3.1 Good practice following recruitment

Following the recruitment of a new employee or volunteer, there are key elements of good practice which should be implemented to ensure the protection of children and young people.

4.3.2 Induction

A well-planned induction programme can help the new employee or volunteer's successful integration into an organisation or group. This programme may include: introductions to colleagues; immediate training in the organisation's child protection policy; explanation of day-to-day processes; clarification of expectations; outlining of conditions and procedures for dealing with discipline and grievances; familiarisation with the ethos of the organisation or group. Familiarisation with lines of management and supervision are particularly important.

4.3.3 Trial or probationary period

Confirmation of appointment should be made subject to the successful completion of a trial or probationary period, the length of which should be decided at the outset (usually six months with a review at three months). This gives an opportunity to assess the suitability of the new member of staff and his or her commitment to the organisation's policies and practices in relation to the safety of children.

4.3.4 Training

All Church personnel should be offered training in child protection policies and procedures, including information about how to respond to suspicions and allegations of child abuse.

To maintain high standards and good practice generally, training should be provided on an ongoing basis. The nature of the training will depend on the range of services provided by the group or organisation and the needs of staff and volunteers.

4.3.5 Supervision and support

Supervision of personnel is an essential part of ensuring the welfare of children and young people. Supervision will include the opportunity to provide feedback and support. This will involve arranging to observe those working with children and young people at regular intervals, on their own or in small groups, and giving members of staff the opportunity to raise any questions they may have, to highlight any problems they are experiencing or to present any suggestions for change that they may wish to make. Supervision also allows managers to assess the need for change in policies or practice, or for additional training.

It is important that supervision procedures include the opportunity to identify and address sources of anxiety or stress for personnel, and for personnel to raise any concerns they may have regarding a child or young person.

4.3.6 Grievance, disciplinary and complaints procedures

Effective grievance, disciplinary and complaints procedures, which seek to resolve difficulties promptly and with fairness,[20] are essential elements of good employment practice.

4.3.7 Written statement of terms

All new employees should receive a written statement of terms of employment, or contract, within two months of commencing employment. This statement will normally include the names and addresses of the employer and employee, a clear job description, hours of work, holidays and sick pay, and reference the organisation's policies on grievance, complaints and disciplinary matters.

On appointment, each person should be given the name of the Director of Child Protection and advised of the role of the Director in relation to child protection procedures. They should also be given a copy of the organisation's Code of Good Practice for working with children and young people.

4.3.8 Policy on the use of computers

Every parish and Church-based organisation shall ensure that it has in place a clear policy regarding the use of email and the internet. The policy should include a clear statement that intentionally using a computer that is the property of a Church organisation or institution to send offensive emails or to receive, view or send pornography of any kind, or other forms of offensive or inappropriate material, will be subject to disciplinary proceedings. These procedures should be clearly described within the policy.

Where it is suspected that a computer in a Church organisation has been used to receive, view or send pornographic images of children or young people, this should be regarded as a child protection issue requiring immediate action in accordance with the procedures for responding to suspicions or allegations of child abuse described in Chapter Eight.

Selection and Formation of Candidates for the Priesthood and Religious Life   **5**

5.1   Introduction

The proper selection and formation of those who present themselves for priesthood and religious life has a vital part to play in ensuring the care and protection of children and young people in the Church. This is true in relation to both the personal formation of candidates and their training in best practice in pastoral engagement with children and young people.

5.2   Selection of Candidates

It is important that those who are accepted into formal training for the priesthood or religious life are determined to have achieved a sufficient level of maturity – particularly affective and emotional maturity – to allow them to engage in and benefit from a programme of formation. In making this determination, the bishop or religious superior shall seek the assistance of those competent in this area, as well as those who know the prospective candidate.

The selection of candidates for priesthood and religious life needs to be seen as an integral process involving the vocational director, the interview board and the bishop or religious superior.

Oral references from responsible people who have known candidates over a long time are also important aids to the selection process. Good examination results, along with school or other references, cannot be considered adequate by themselves.

5.3   Formation[21]

5.3.1   Personal formation

In keeping with the recommendations of a number of Church documents,[22] the programme of formation shall include a sound human formation and draw on the insights of the human sciences.

It is particularly important that the process of formation fosters the growth and integration of the affective life of the individual, including his or her sexuality in the context of a celibate lifestyle.

It is also essential that formation personnel are satisfied that the future priest or religious can relate appropriately both to children and adults before presenting him or her for ordination or final vows.

5.3.2 Training in best practice

Those in formation for priesthood and the religious life shall be given comprehensive training in safe and best practice in working with children and young people.

This training will include, at the earliest possible stage, the provision of clear information about how to respond if concerns about child protection arise in the context of formation or outside it. All those in formation shall be provided with the name and contact details of the relevant Director of Child Protection and shall be made aware of the procedures for reporting suspicions or allegations of child abuse outlined in this document. They shall be made aware of the commitment in the Church's procedures to act in accordance with the principle that the welfare of children is always the paramount consideration.

Other issues which should be covered in formation include the absolute importance of respecting appropriate boundaries in interaction with children; knowledge of the theories associated with sexual abuse, how abusers operate and the elements of treatment for abusers; awareness of the immediate and long-term impact of abuse of all kinds, and the pastoral needs of all those affected by child abuse.

The placement of a candidate for the priesthood or religious life in pastoral situations allows those responsible for formation to observe and assess the ability of candidates to relate to those with whom they will be expected to minister following ordination or profession. Facilitating candidates with opportunities to reflect on their pastoral experience and to learn from it is intrinsic to the formation process.

Placement in any pastoral situation that involves working with children and young people requires careful planning, supervision and assessment. The vetting procedures in the relevant jurisdiction should be utilised. Candidates should expect and receive the same formal supervision as other trainees and staff.

It is essential that those entrusted with the formation of priests and religious are themselves properly trained in the area of child protection and that their work with those in formation is adequately supported and supervised.

Similarly, sound pastoral and professional practice suggests that in the early years of ministry it is important to provide for:

- ongoing pastoral supervision;
- continuing professional development;
- a system of personal support and mentoring;
- periodic personal reviews of experience in ministry

5.4 Transfer from other Dioceses and Jurisdictions

Visiting clergy and religious may come to a parish for various reasons, including, for example, taking on a full-time appointment, providing cover in the absence of a priest of the parish, leading a parish retreat or mission, or making an 'appeal'. The Church's responsibility for the safety and well-being of children and young people includes ensuring that proper procedures are in place in relation to visiting clergy and religious.

Each diocese and religious congregation shall apply the following principles and procedures:

- Prior to permitting any priest or religious to take up an appointment, a bishop or religious superior shall seek detailed information about the suitability of the person for ministry from his or her sending bishop or religious superior, whether from inside or outside of the country. (See Appendix Eight and Appendix Nine.)
- The sending bishop or religious superior shall in turn assess and indicate clearly to the receiving bishop or religious superior the suitability of the priest or religious proposed for assignment or incardination. This assessment shall be based upon the personal knowledge of the bishop or religious superior of the person concerned, upon a review of the written record of the person proposed for ministry and upon enquiry among other knowledgeable persons who are able to offer an assessment of the suitability of the priest or religious for ministry in the receiving diocese or religious congregation.
- In particular, this assessment will clearly indicate whether the priest or religious proposed for ministry has previously exhibited any behaviour which would indicate that they are a risk to children or which could be considered in any other way improper. The failure to provide such information shall be considered sufficient grounds to deny a request for permission to minister in the receiving diocese or religious congregation, or to transfer.
- All visiting priests and religious shall be made aware of the Code of Good Practice for working with children and young people operating in the parish or organisation in which they will be ministering and shall be asked to give an undertaking that they will abide by it.
- Every bishop and religious superior shall undertake to ensure that no priest or religious who has been deemed to have committed any form of child abuse is transferred for ministry.

PART THREE

Responding to Allegations and Suspicions of Child Abuse

Part Three of *Our Children, Our Church* outlines procedures to be followed when an allegation or suspicion of child abuse comes to the attention of Church personnel.

Chapter Six sets out key elements of a response to allegations or suspicions of child abuse.

Chapter Seven summarises the definitions, provided in the civil guidelines, of the various forms of child abuse.

Chapter Eight outlines the steps to be taken when an allegation or suspicion arises, including the procedure to be followed when reporting to the civil authorities.

Chapter Nine describes actions to be taken by a Church organisation following the reporting of an allegation or suspicion.

Chapter Ten deals with canon law procedures where an allegation of child abuse concerns a priest or religious.

Chapter Eleven relates to the outcome of investigations by the civil authorities.

Chapter Twelve outlines issues relating to future risk where priests or religious are convicted of child abuse or where there are continuing concerns.

Chapter Thirteen deals with responding to the pastoral needs of those who have been affected by child abuse by Church personnel.

6 Key Elements of a Response

6.1 Introduction

The Church's response to allegations and suspicions of child abuse will be informed by the guiding principles set out in Chapter One, principles that include the paramount importance of ensuring the child's right to safety and care; the right of those who have suffered abuse to a just and compassionate response; the right of an accused person to a fair process which respects natural justice. In addition, there are a number of key elements in an appropriate response to alleged or suspected child abuse, which are outlined below.

6.2 An Inter-Agency Approach

The management and appropriate handling of child protection and welfare is a skilled and delicate task which requires knowledge, expertise and sensitivity. It also requires a coordinated and inter-agency approach. Such an approach ensures effective use of the breadth of expertise that is located in different agencies, communication between those necessarily involved, clarity of respective roles, information-sharing, pooling of resources, a comprehensive response and mutual support.

The roles of State agencies involved in the safety and protection of children and young people – the Government, the Health Service Executive in the Republic of Ireland, Health and Social Services Boards and Trusts in Northern Ireland, An Garda Síochána and the Police Service of Northern Ireland (PSNI) – are outlined in Appendix Ten.

6.3 Exchange of Information

The exchange of information between all relevant agencies is a key element in safeguarding the welfare of children and in providing an appropriate response where child abuse occurs. Effective communication between Church organisations and the civil authorities is therefore essential.

6.4 Referring Child Abuse to the Civil Authorities

While mandatory reporting is not provided for in the legislation of either the Republic of Ireland or Northern Ireland, the civil policies in both jurisdictions place an obligation on all adults and organisations to report child abuse to the civil authorities.

6.5 Reasonable Grounds for Concern

The civil guidelines emphasise that where any person encounters a situation which gives rise to concern that a child has been, or is being, abused, or is at risk of abuse, the matter should be reported to the civil authorities. *Children First* states:

> The following examples would constitute reasonable grounds for concern:
> i. specific indication from the child that (s)he was abused;
> ii. an account by a person who saw the child being abused;
> iii. evidence, such as an injury or behaviour, which is consistent with abuse and unlikely to be caused in any other way;
> iv. an injury or behaviour which is consistent both with abuse and with an innocent explanation but where there are corroborative indicators supporting the concern that it may be a case of abuse. An example of this would be a pattern of injuries, an implausible explanation, other indications of abuse, dysfunctional behaviour;
> v. consistent indication, over a period of time, that a child is suffering from emotional or physical neglect.[23]

6.6 Existing Procedures

Many Church-based organisations, within the health and education sectors in particular, come under the direct responsibility of government agencies which have specified child protection policies, including procedures for reporting allegations and suspicions of child abuse. For such organisations, their existing procedures, rather than those in this document, are to be followed.

6.7 Confidentiality

The relationship of Church personnel with children and young people in their care is based on trust and confidentiality.[24] There may be times, however, when a child or a young person – or indeed an adult – confides in a person who works for the Church information which indicates that child abuse may have occurred or that the safety of children or young people is at risk, and they may ask that the matter be treated as completely confidential. In this situation, the person working for the Church should carefully explain that although they respect the sensitive nature of the information, they are unable to give an assurance of complete confidentiality: they will need to inform the relevant authorities so that action may be taken to protect children and young people from potential harm.

Children First highlights key issues in regard to confidentiality as follows:

- All information regarding concerns about child abuse should be shared on a 'need to know' basis in the best interests of children.[25]
- No undertakings regarding secrecy can be given.[26] This should be made clear to all parties involved. Giving information to others for the protection of a child is not a breach of confidentiality.
- Information obtained for one purpose must not be used for another without consulting the person who provided that information.[27]

6.7.1 The Seal of Confession

The maintenance of trust in the Sacrament of Reconciliation requires the guarantee of absolute confidentiality, allowing for no exceptions. This is known as the Seal of Confession and guarantees to the penitent that anything revealed to the confessor will not be divulged to anyone else (canon 983). It is not desirable for the confessor to undertake to divulge matters revealed in confession, even when the penitent gives consent.

Pastoral wisdom would advise that in the event of a child or young person disclosing in confession that they have been abused, the confessor should sensitively reassure the child or young person that they are not at fault. The confessor should encourage the child or young person to disclose the abuse to an adult they trust (for example, a relative, teacher, friend) and to have that person report the abuse. The confessor must at no time act in any manner that might violate the seal or compromise the Sacrament of Reconciliation in the eyes of the faithful.

When an abuser confesses to a priest previously undisclosed child abuse, the priest should advise the penitent to seek the professional help they require immediately, for their own well-being and in order to prevent any recurrence of abuse.

6.8 Prompt and Appropriate Response

It is imperative that those who receive allegations of child abuse, or have suspicions that abuse may have occurred, should act promptly and sensitively. However, they should not exceed their role in any way. Neither children nor parents should be interviewed in detail about the alleged abuse.

6.9 Recording of Information

Where child abuse is alleged or suspected, it is vital that the person who receives the allegation, or who suspects abuse, records in writing, as accurately as possible, what has been revealed. The written record should include all the relevant information that has been disclosed or observed, including, for example, dates, times, names, locations and context.

7.1 Introduction

In considering child protection issues, it is necessary to understand the nature of child abuse, its different forms, how to recognise it and what steps to take when it is encountered. The aim of this chapter is to give an overview of the definitions of child abuse outlined in the civil guidelines so as to enable Church personnel to be alert to the indicators of possible abuse.

7.2 What is Child Abuse?

Child abuse occurs when the behaviour of someone in a position of greater power than a child or young person abuses that power and causes harm to that child or young person. The common denominator of all child abuse is that it makes children and young people feel diminished or threatened, and that it causes them harm. All forms of child abuse constitute a betrayal of trust and an abuse of power by an adult over a child or young person.

Child abuse is generally categorised into four broad groups: neglect, emotional abuse, physical abuse and sexual abuse. Consistent with civil guidelines in both jurisdictions, all forms of child abuse are covered in this document.

Each form of child abuse must be treated seriously; there can be no suggestion that some forms are of less significance than others. Accounts from survivors and child care experts have pointed to the devastating and long-lasting effects that any form of child abuse can have on children and young people and how these effects can continue long into adulthood.

It is accepted, however, that there is a distinction between sexual abuse and other ways in which children can be harmed in that the motivation and circumstances for the sexual abuse of children can be very different from those which are involved when people physically or emotionally abuse children, or cause them to be neglected.

7.3 Forms of Child[28] Abuse

Children may be abused in a range of settings, by those known to them or, more rarely, by a stranger.[29] As already noted, there are four principal categories of child abuse – neglect, emotional abuse, physical abuse and sexual abuse – and a child may be subject to more than one form at any time during his or her childhood. (See list of indicators of the various forms of child abuse, Appendix Eleven.)

7.3.1 Neglect

Neglect can be defined in terms of an omission, where the child suffers significant harm or impairment of development by being deprived of food, clothing, warmth, hygiene, intellectual stimulation, supervision and safety, attachment to and affection from adults, and medical care.[30]

Neglect generally becomes apparent in different ways over a period of time rather than at one specific point.[31] It is the persistent failure to meet a child's physical, emotional and/or psychological needs that is likely to result in significant harm.[32]

Examples of neglect include:

- Where a child suffers a series of minor injuries as a result of not being properly supervised or protected.
- The consistent failure of a child to gain weight or height may indicate that they are being deprived of adequate nutrition.
- Where a child consistently misses school, this may be due to bullying or deprivation of intellectual stimulation and support.[33]

7.3.2 Emotional abuse

Emotional abuse is the persistent emotional ill-treatment of a child such as to cause severe and persistent adverse effects on the child's emotional development.[34]

Emotional abuse is normally found in the relationship between a care-giver and a child rather than in a specific event or pattern of events. It occurs when a child's need for affection, approval, consistency and security is not met. Unless other forms of abuse are present, it is rarely manifested in physical signs or symptoms.[35]

7.3.3 Physical abuse

Physical abuse is any form of non-accidental injury, or injury which results from wilful or neglectful failure to protect a child. Examples of physical injury include the following:

- shaking a child;
- using excessive force in handling;
- deliberate poisoning;
- suffocation;
- allowing or creating a substantial risk of significant harm to a child.[36]

7.3.4 Sexual abuse

Sexual abuse occurs when a child is used by another person for his or her gratification or sexual arousal, or for that of others.[37] Any form of sexual behaviour engaged in by an adult with a child or young person is sexual abuse, and is both immoral and criminal.[38]

There may also be 'indirect abuse' of children, for instance, where children have been photographed, videotaped or filmed for pornographic purposes.[39] Indirect abuse also includes the subjecting of children to gross and obscene language or indecent images. The use or possession of child pornography in any form is illegal and there is an obligation to report information concerning anyone possessing such material to the police authorities.

7.4 Children with Special Vulnerabilities

The civil guidelines pay particular attention to children with special vulnerabilities. These are children who, for one reason or another, may be more vulnerable to abuse than others. They could include children with disabilities; children who are separated from their parents or other family members and are reliant on others for their care and protection, either in foster care or residential settings; and homeless children. The same categories of abuse as described above are applicable but may take a slightly different form. For example, abuse may take the form of deprivation of basic rights, harsh disciplinary regimes or the inappropriate use of medications or physical restraints.[40]

7.5 Peer Abuse

In some instances of child abuse, the alleged abuser may be another child or young person. In such situations, there are important child protection issues in relation to both children and the needs of each should be considered separately.[41] The civil authorities should be notified of such cases.

8 Initial Response and Reporting Procedures

8.1 Introduction

This chapter deals with the initial response to allegations or suspicions of child abuse which come to the notice of personnel working within the Church, and with the procedures for reporting allegations or suspicions to the civil authorities.

What follows is concerned primarily with allegations or suspicions involving Church personnel (clergy, religious, lay employees or volunteers). However, since people who work for the Church may also encounter allegations or suspicions of child abuse that do not involve Church personnel, some general guidance for this situation is also given (see Section 8.10).

8.2 Importance of Procedures

Those who experience child abuse and who disclose it to a person working for the Church have a right to expect a sensitive, prompt and appropriate response. The existence of clear procedures which are known and understood by Church personnel can help to ensure that such a response is provided.

For those working in the Church, the experience of encountering an allegation or suspicion of child abuse can be deeply distressing and can have a profound effect on them as individuals, as well as on their organisation or group. Clear procedures, together with training and supports, will help to equip people to deal with the situation in a calm, sensitive, fair and appropriate manner.[42]

8.3 Supports and Structures within the Church

As described in Chapter Two (Section 2.3.3), each bishop, religious superior and chairperson of a Church organisation will have available to them a Director of Child Protection who acts on their behalf and who provides professional expertise, advice and support in relation to matters of child protection. The Director of Child Protection is a professionally trained person whose function corresponds to that of the Designated Person outlined in the civil guidelines; he or she has responsibility for referring allegations and suspicions of child abuse involving Church personnel and for implementing the appropriate procedures.

Each parish (or cluster of parishes) will have a nominated Parish Child Protection Representative (Section 2.5.2) who will facilitate and support anyone in the parish in bringing an allegation or suspicion to the attention of the Director of Child Protection, should they wish to have such support.

8.4   Encountering Allegations or Suspicions

Child abuse may come to light in a number of different ways. In essence, it may be alleged or suspected. An allegation of child abuse is direct, specific and supported by some sort of evidence. In this document, the term 'allegation' may include the following situations:

- Where a person, either an adult or a child, alleges that they have been abused and they name the alleged perpetrator.
- Where a person alleges that they have been abused but are unable or are unwilling to name the perpetrator.
- Where a person alleges that they have been abused but the perpetrator has died.
- Where a person reveals that another person has told them of being abused; or where they themselves have witnessed abuse.

A suspicion is less direct or specific. However, in either case, it is necessary to take further action. The specific procedures for dealing with allegations are outlined in Section 8.6; the procedures for dealing with suspicions are in Section 8.7.

8.5   The Church's Dual Responsibility

When an allegation or suspicion of child abuse arises in relation to a person working for the Church, the Church organisation holds a dual responsibility:

- *The safeguarding of children:* this at all times must take priority. The Church organisation must ensure that all appropriate procedures are followed in relation to reporting the matter to the civil authorities and it must do all within its power to ensure that no child continues to be exposed to the risk of being abused.
- *Dealing with the person accused:* the Church organisation must ensure that proper procedures are followed in relation to the person against whom the complaint has been made, in line with both fair procedures and natural justice. The accused person should be treated as innocent unless the contrary is established.

8.6 Procedures for Responding to Allegations of Child Abuse

8.6.1 First response on receiving an allegation

Where a child or young person discloses child abuse to a person working in any capacity in the Church, it is important that the situation is handled sensitively and compassionately. It should be borne in mind that the child or young person may feel they have taken a huge risk in disclosing the abuse.

The following general guidance should be observed:

- The person receiving the allegation should remain calm and not show an extreme reaction. They should listen to the child or young person with sensitivity and understanding; they should facilitate them to tell about the problem, but avoid interviewing them.
- The person receiving the allegation should be conscious that the child may feel very frightened and need reassurance and support that they have done the right thing in disclosing the abuse.
- It should be made clear that the person receiving the allegation is not in a position to promise to keep the information secret. However, reassurance can be given that it will be treated as confidential and will be shared only with those who have a right to hear it.
- The person receiving the disclosure should avoid appearing judgemental about the person against whom the allegation is being made.
- The child or young person should not be questioned unless the nature of what is being said is unclear. It may be necessary to clarify that what was said has been correctly understood, but leading questions should be avoided.
- The steps that are likely to follow should be explained to the child or young person.
- Parents or guardians should be informed unless to do so would place the child at further risk.

In the case of an adult disclosing child abuse, it is equally important that the initial response is characterised by compassion and sensitivity. The general guidance outlined above should be followed.

The person who receives an allegation of child abuse should actively encourage the person who is making it to report the matter to the civil authorities. Appropriate arrangements should be made to support them in doing so, if this is what they wish. Should the person making the allegation be under eighteen years of age, their parent or guardian can make a statement on their behalf.

Whether or not the person making the allegation wishes to report it to the civil authorities, it should be explained to them that the Church's child protection procedures require that the allegation be referred to the Church's Director of Child Protection. The procedures that are likely to follow should also be explained.

The person receiving the allegation should record in writing all relevant information received, including, for example, dates, times, names, locations and context.

They should then inform the Director of Child Protection of the allegation.

All allegations of child abuse against Church personnel shall be reported without delay to the Church's Director of Child Protection, who is the Designated Person to receive allegations and suspicions, and who acts on behalf of the bishop or religious superior.

8.6.2 Role of the Director of Child Protection

The Director of Child Protection shall immediately inform the bishop or religious superior (or, in their absence, the person acting in their place) or, in the case of lay personnel, the chairperson of the Church organisation, of the allegation.

When an allegation of child abuse is received, the Director of Child Protection, as the Designated Person, shall determine whether there are 'reasonable grounds for concern' that child abuse may have occurred and shall proceed in one of the following ways. Before proceeding, the Director of Child Protection shall inform the bishop or religious superior or chairperson of what is proposed.

1. Report directly to the civil authorities

Where it is established that there are reasonable grounds for concern that child abuse has occurred, the Director of Child Protection shall, on behalf of the bishop or religious superior, or chairperson of the Church organisation, report the allegation to the civil authorities immediately. In the Republic of Ireland, the report should be made to the appropriate Health Service Executive area and copied to An Garda Síochána. In Northern Ireland, the report should be made to the appropriate Health and Social Services Trust, and copied to the PSNI. The Director of Child Protection shall also inform the bishop or religious superior or chairperson of the Church organisation in writing that this report to the civil authorities has been made.

In reporting these matters, the Director will have satisfied him or herself that there is at least a semblance of truth to the allegation.

2. Seek further clarification

The Director of Child Protection may need to seek greater clarification and further information in establishing whether 'reasonable grounds for concern' exist.

Where there is any uncertainty, then the procedure for considering suspicions of child abuse should be followed (Section 8.7 below).[43]

3. Take no further action against the accused person

This will only occur where the Director of Child Protection is satisfied immediately that it would have been impossible for the person complained of to have committed the alleged action or offence, for example where it was established that he or she was absent from the alleged location (perhaps out of the country) at the time that the alleged offence took place.

Where no further action is to be taken, it will be the responsibility of the Director of Child Protection to:

- Advise the complainant in writing of the action taken on foot of the complaint and its outcome, including information on other means of pursuing their complaint if they remain dissatisfied.
- Keep a record of the complaint indicating its nature, when, by whom and to whom it was made, and a brief explanation of why it was considered that no further action should be taken, together with any correspondence on the case.
- Advise the accused person that a complaint has been made and inform them of its nature; advise them that it is considered to be without substance and that no further action is being taken. Appropriate support should be offered.
- Consider whether the child or young person may have been abused by someone else and, if necessary, report the matter to the civil authorities for follow-up.

8.7 Procedures for Responding to Suspicions of Child Abuse

8.7.1 Response of the person who has suspicions

A suspicion that a child or young person is at risk of abuse or is being abused is less direct or specific than an allegation. A person might, for example, become suspicious as a result of rumours; anonymous claims; signs of behavioural, psychological or emotional change; fear on the part of a child or young person; contact with a known abuser; unexplained injury.

Where suspicions of child abuse arise, and the suspected person is working for the Church, the person who encounters the suspicion must record the details in writing and refer the matter to the Director of Child Protection immediately.

Even when a person has suspicions but is not sure if child abuse is involved, they should nevertheless record the details and refer the matter to the Director of Child Protection without delay.

8.7.2 Role of the Director of Child Protection

When the suspicion has been referred to the Director of Child Protection, he or she will examine whether 'reasonable grounds for concern' exist. The following would constitute 'reasonable grounds for concern':

- Evidence, such as an injury or behaviour, which is consistent with abuse and unlikely to be caused in any other way.
- An injury or behaviour which is consistent both with abuse and with an innocent explanation but where there are corroborative indicators supporting the concern that it may be a case of abuse. An example of this would be a pattern of injuries, an implausible explanation, other indications of abuse and/or dysfunctional behaviour.
- Consistent indication over a period of time that a child is suffering emotional or physical neglect.[44]

A suspicion which is not supported by any objective indication of abuse or neglect would not constitute a reasonable suspicion or reasonable grounds for concern.[45]

If it is established that reasonable grounds for concern do exist, the Director of Child Protection shall inform the bishop or religious superior or chairperson of the Church organisation and then report the matter without delay to the civil authorities – the Health Service Executive area in the Republic of Ireland or Health and Social Services Trust in Northern Ireland, and copy the report to An Garda Síochána or the PSNI.

Where there is any doubt or uncertainty, but concerns remain, the Director of Child Protection will, without delay, consult with the civil authorities on the appropriate steps to be taken.[46]

The Director of Child Protection will keep a written record of the outcome of the consultation with the civil authorities.

The outcome of the consultation may be that it is established that reasonable grounds for concern do exist. In this case, the Director of Child Protection shall inform the bishop or religious superior or chairperson of the Church organisation and make a formal report of the suspicion to the civil authorities.

It may be decided following the consultation that there are no grounds for the Director of Child Protection to formally report the matter to the civil authorities. In this case, the person who referred the matter should be given a written statement by the Director of Child Protection outlining the reasons no further action is being taken and indicating that, if they remain concerned about the situation, they are free to consult with, or report to, the civil authorities themselves.[47]

8.8   Historical Allegations

Those who have been abused in their childhood may not actually disclose the abuse until many years, or even decades, later. It is Church policy to create a caring and responsive atmosphere in which people can disclose child abuse, regardless of how long ago it took place.

A person who approaches the Church concerning abuse in the past should receive a prompt, compassionate and sensitive response. In addition, the child protection implications of the complaint must be treated with as much urgency as those arising from allegations of current or recent child abuse. This is because there may be a continuing risk to children and young people by the person against whom the allegation has been made.[48]

The following procedures shall apply in respect of all historical allegations of child abuse:

- The policies and procedures for responding to allegations of current or recent abuse must be fully operated for historical cases which come to the attention of Church personnel, in particular in regard to the reporting procedures (as outlined in Section 8.6 above), dealing with the alleged abuser (Chapters Nine and Ten) and pastoral interaction with the person making the complaint (Chapter Thirteen).
- Where an adult discloses abuse they experienced as a child or young person, they should be encouraged and supported to report the matter directly to the civil authorities. Whether or not the person making the allegation wishes to report it to the civil authorities, it should be explained to them that the Director of Child Protection must nevertheless be informed of the allegation, as there may be implications for the current safety of children or young people, or for the investigation of historical allegations made by others.

- The Director of Child Protection, after informing the bishop or religious superior or chairperson of the Church organisation, and having established that there are 'reasonable grounds for concern' that child abuse has occurred, must report the allegation to the civil authorities in accordance with the procedures in Section 8.6 of this chapter.
- Where historical allegations arise in the course of civil or other enquiries and these have not been already referred to the authorities, they should be reported using the procedures outlined in Section 8.6.
- Similarly, previous allegations of child abuse that were known to Church personnel in the past but were not reported at the time they were received should be dealt with in this way.
- Where the person against whom the allegation is being made is deceased, the police authorities should still be informed as there may be implications for the investigation of other cases.
- It is possible that, due to lapse of time, third party disclosures of some historical cases may not provide sufficient information to assess if there are 'reasonable grounds for concern' that child abuse occurred. In these instances, the process detailed above regarding suspicions of abuse (Section 8.7) should be followed.

8.9 Inappropriate Behaviour and Misconduct

There may be instances where, in the judgement of the Director of Child Protection, the complaint does not constitute 'reasonable grounds for concern' that child abuse has occurred, but rather indicates inappropriate behaviour, misconduct or a breach of standards on the part of the person in question. In such instances, it may be necessary for the bishop, religious superior or chairperson of the Church organisation to take further action and/or implement disciplinary procedures.[49] Such action might include obtaining a professional assessment of fitness to carry out duties; advice and counselling; a requirement to undertake special training or seek specialised assistance.[50]

8.10 Allegations or Suspicions not Involving Church Personnel

In situations where a person working within the Church has concerns that a child or young person with whom they have contact is at risk of or is experiencing child abuse, either within or outside their family, they have a civil and moral responsibility to report the matter directly to the civil authorities, as outlined in *Children First*[51] and *Co-operating to Safeguard Children*.[52] It is the role of the civil authorities to assess the situation and to take action to safeguard the child or young person, if required.

9 Post-Reporting Issues

9.1 Introduction

As indicated in Chapter Eight (Section 8.5), a Church organisation holds a dual responsibility when an allegation or suspicion of child abuse arises: to ensure that children are protected and that the accused person is dealt with appropriately.[53]

The Director of Child Protection has specific responsibilities in regard to child protection issues, including the reporting of allegations and suspicions to the civil authorities (Sections 8.6 and 8.7). Issues in regard to the accused person are the particular responsibility of the bishop, religious superior or chairperson of the Church organisation, depending on whether the accused person is a priest, religious or lay employee or volunteer.

9.2 Actions Following Reporting

9.2.1 Consultation with civil authorities

Once an allegation or suspicion of child abuse has been reported to the civil authorities and the bishop, religious superior or chairperson has been informed, the Director of Child Protection will arrange an initial meeting with the civil authorities as a matter of urgency.

This meeting will look at the child protection issues arising from the allegation or suspicion of child abuse with a view to ensuring that no child is exposed to unnecessary risk. The meeting will consider protective measures: such measures should be proportionate to the level of risk and should not unreasonably penalise the person accused, financially or otherwise.[54]

The meeting will also consider the manner and timing by which the person concerned is informed that an accusation of child abuse has been made against them and has been reported to the civil authorities. While the timing must take into account the need to ensure that it in no way endangers a child, or enables the accused person to interfere with the civil investigation, a person against whom an allegation is made should in natural justice be informed as soon as possible.

Where the civil authorities ask that there be a delay in informing the accused person, the Director of Child Protection should seek written confirmation of the request.

9.2.2 Meeting with the bishop, religious superior or chairperson

Immediately after the meeting with the civil authorities, the Director of Child Protection will inform the bishop, religious superior or chairperson of its deliberations regarding: the level of risk posed to children; actions in relation to the accused person pending the outcome of the civil investigation, and the question of informing the accused person.

9.3 Next Stages in Procedures: Priests or Religious

If the person against whom the allegation is made is a priest or religious, then the procedures outlined in Chapter Ten should be followed.

9.4 Next Stages in Procedures: Lay Employees or Volunteers

9.4.1 Informing the accused person

Following the meeting between the Director of Child Protection and the chairperson (Section 9.2.2), the chairperson should advise the person accused of the allegation, in accordance with the proposal about timing made in the consultation with the civil authorities (Section 9.2.1).

The chairperson will:

- Communicate a summary of the allegation to the accused person.
- Remind them of their right not to respond to or to admit to any offence.
- Ensure that they understand that anything they say may be introduced as evidence in court.
- Ask the accused person to meet with the Director of Child Protection to hear the details of the allegation.

The chairperson will also encourage the accused person to obtain legal advice and counselling support as soon as possible.

9.4.2 Administrative leave

The consultations between the Director of Child Protection and the civil authorities (Section 9.2.1) may have recommended that the accused person be required to 'step aside' or take 'administrative leave'.

If this is the case, the chairperson will inform the accused person of the recommendation and explain to them that the taking of such leave is a standard procedure in employment settings and organisations while an investigation is underway and is not an indication of guilt. Any person who is asked to take such leave is still entitled to his or her rightful income and his or her right to be provided with a residence (where applicable).

While a request to take administrative leave may cause significant distress, it may be an essential and precautionary process to protect children and to allow time to establish if there is a basis to an allegation or suspicion of child abuse.

The right to natural justice and presumption of innocence must be preserved.

9.4.3 Other considerations

Given the gravity of an allegation of child abuse, care must be taken by employers, relevant management committees, and any others involved in dealing with the matter, to ensure that any communication with the person accused, or with their colleagues, or other associates, is clear and non-judgemental. The presumption of innocence must be preserved until guilt or responsibility is proven and the principles of natural justice must be respected. The accused person should be dealt with in a sensitive and compassionate manner.

Employers or managers should take care to ensure that actions taken by them do not undermine or frustrate any investigations being conducted by the civil authorities.

While an investigation is in progress, the chairperson of the Church organisation, or the person so delegated, will remain in contact with the Director of Child Protection in regard to any ongoing child protection issues. The Director of Child Protection should, in turn, consult with the civil authorities as required.

Aspects of dealing with allegations or suspicions of child abuse concerning employees or volunteers can vary considerably from case to case and it may therefore be appropriate for a Church organisation to seek legal advice.

10.1 Introduction

In parallel with its duties regarding the reporting of allegations or suspicions of child abuse to the civil authorities, the Church will also implement the procedures required by canon law where an allegation or suspicion concerns a diocesan priest, religious cleric, lay religious,[55] bishop or religious superior.

Canon law confers on bishops and on religious superiors the authority to act decisively in relation to any risk posed to children; they exercise both the responsibility and competence to do whatever is necessary to ensure the welfare of children. 'Ecclesiastical authority is entitled to regulate, in view of the common good, the exercise of rights which are proper to Christ's faithful.'[56] The regulation of these rights shall always hold as paramount the welfare of children.

If a doubt exists as to whether a person is deemed to pose a risk to the welfare of children, bishops and religious superiors have the authority to restrict the ministry of a cleric as long as this situation prevails. This is a precautionary administrative procedure taken for the common good.

Care should be taken to ensure that any canonical procedure does not undermine a civil investigation.

Canon law has particular procedures relating to sexual abuse, with specific requirements arising when the accused person is:

- a diocesan priest or religious cleric (Section 10.2);
- a lay religious (Section 10.3);
- a bishop or religious superior (Section 10.4).

When the allegation relates to abuse which is other than sexual abuse, different procedures apply. These are outlined in Section 10.5.

10.2 Procedures Relating to Diocesan Priests and Religious Clergy

10.2.1 Introduction

The canonical procedure outlined below must be followed when an allegation of child sexual abuse is made against a diocesan priest or a religious cleric.

10.2.2 Responsibilities of the Ordinary[57]

Following the meeting between the Director of Child Protection and the civil authorities (Section 9.2.1), the Ordinary will meet the cleric in person and inform him that an allegation has been received and that it is being dealt with in accordance with the Church's policies and procedures for the protection of children. The manner and timing by which the Ordinary is to inform the accused cleric is to be guided by the conclusions of the meeting between the Director of Child Protection and the civil authorities, bearing in mind the rights in natural justice of the cleric who is accused.

On communicating the allegation:

- The Ordinary will provide a summary of the substance of the allegation to the accused cleric.
- The Ordinary will remind the accused cleric of his right not to respond to or admit to any offence and his right to legal representation and a canonical advisor.
- The Ordinary will ensure that the accused cleric understands that anything he says may be introduced as evidence in a canonical or civil court.
- The Ordinary cannot request the accused cleric to confess, sacramentally or non-sacramentally, to the allegation, nor should the Ordinary hear the sacramental confession of the accused cleric.
- The Ordinary will ask the accused cleric to meet the Director of Child Protection to hear the details of the allegation as soon as he has chosen a legal and canonical advisor.

In addition, the Ordinary will provide a list of Support Persons who will be available to meet the accused cleric to offer him pastoral support. The Support Person may be a lay person, or a priest or religious.

The Ordinary will also provide the accused cleric with a list of canonical advisors but will respect the right of the accused cleric to choose a canonical advisor other than one of those listed.

The Ordinary will explain that pastoral care will be offered to the accused person's family.

The Ordinary will direct the accused cleric, and any person representing him, to have no contact prior to the completion of an investigation with the person who has made the allegation, their family or the person who brought forward the allegation. This shall be communicated by means of a Precept.[58]

If the accused cleric is not incardinated in the diocese in which the allegation originates, the bishop will inform the accused cleric's Ordinary. With this communication the bishop will request that the accused cleric's Ordinary direct, by Precept, the cleric and those acting on his behalf not to have any contact prior to the completion of the investigation with the complainant, their family or the person who brought forward the allegation. A copy of the Precept is to be sent to the bishop of the diocese in which the allegation originates.

The Ordinary is to convene a meeting with the Child Protection Committee of the diocese or religious congregation as soon as possible, to assist him in the ongoing response to the allegation.

10.2.3 Preliminary investigation

When the Ordinary receives information, which has at least the semblance of truth, from the Director of Child Protection or any other source, about an allegation of sexual abuse by a cleric, he will decree the initiation of a preliminary investigation, unless this inquiry would appear to be entirely superfluous (canon 1717, §1). This is without prejudice to any civil investigation.

When the Ordinary determines that sufficient evidence has been gathered to initiate a canonical process, he will issue a written decree closing the preliminary investigation, with the reason for his determination at least summarily expressed.

If the result of the preliminary investigation is that the accusation is credible, the Ordinary must refer the case to the Congregation for the Doctrine of the Faith.

10.2.4 Responsibilities of the Director of Child Protection

The Director of Child Protection will meet the accused cleric to inform him of the name of the person who made the allegation, and provide details of the allegation.

In the event of the accused cleric not yet having chosen one, a Support Person will be made available to him.

The Director of Child Protection will remind the accused cleric of his right not to respond to the allegation or admit to any offence, and that he is not required to implicate or incriminate himself.

If the accused cleric has not already sought out legal or canonical advisors, the Director of Child Protection will remind him of his right to legal representation and to a canonical advisor.

It may be necessary for the meeting to be adjourned to facilitate this process. The accused cleric will be offered appropriate help in obtaining this legal and/or canonical assistance. The accused cleric may choose a canonical advisor from the information provided for him by the Director of Child Protection, or he may choose his own.

A notary shall be present to minute the meeting between the Director of Child Protection and the accused cleric.

10.2.5 Leave from ministry for diocesan or religious clergy

Leaving intact the rights of the accused cleric to hold a particular ecclesiastical office, the Ordinary can ask the accused cleric to voluntarily refrain from the exercise of that office, and from other forms of public ministry, including the public celebration of the Mass and other sacraments, for the duration of the investigation of the allegation.

Where there is a risk that an accused cleric could abuse children or young people but he cannot be persuaded to stand aside from office, if knowledge of the allegation renders a cleric's ministry ineffective or if his continuing ministry would constitute a scandal to the faithful, the ministry of the accused cleric should, for the good of the Church (*pro bono Ecclesiae*), be immediately limited. The Ordinary can proceed by taking disciplinary action (canons 192–193, 1740–44, 552) and/or decree the removal of the faculties of a cleric (for example, to hear confession, to preach or to preside at marriages) for the duration of the investigation. Where necessary, the Ordinary may issue the cleric with a penal Precept requiring him to stand aside from ministry on the pain of incurring a determined penalty (canon 1319, §2).

In the case of a religious cleric, the major religious superior, in accordance with the Constitutions of each institute, will require the accused cleric to take leave from public ministry, pending the outcome of the civil investigation of the complaint. Where necessary, a diocesan bishop can remove a religious from a position in accordance with canon 682, §2.

An accused cleric who is asked to take leave from ministry is still entitled to his rightful income and his right to be provided with a residence. Any deprivation of these rights at this stage is to be interpreted as punitive and can be the subject of canonical recourse to the Congregation for the Doctrine of the Faith.

The accused cleric may be requested to seek an appropriate medical or psychological evaluation at a mutually acceptable facility. This assessment will be carried out by an accredited professional and a contract will be agreed with regard to its future use. However an accused cleric cannot be forced to undergo this evaluation. If an accused cleric undergoes an evaluation, the results may not be released without his consent.

The fact that an accused cleric is asked to take leave from ministry is not to be understood as determination of his guilt, nor is the acceptance of the request to be considered an admission of guilt, always mindful of the presumption of innocence of the accused cleric until proven guilty and of the fundamental right of every person to their good name.

The accused cleric is to be given the opportunity to express a view regarding how he wishes the fact of his leave from ministry to be communicated to the clergy of his diocese or his fellow religious, his family and any other person he may wish to be informed.

At any point, an accused cleric may voluntarily resign from his ministerial position.

At any point, an accused cleric may request from the Roman Pontiff a dispensation from the obligations of the clerical state (laicisation).

10.3 Procedures Relating to Religious who are not Ordained

10.3.1 Introduction

The canonical procedure outlined below must be followed when an allegation of child sexual abuse is made against a member of a religious institute, society of apostolic life or secular institute who is not ordained.

10.3.2 Responsibilities of the Major Religious Superior[59]

Following the meeting between the Director of Child Protection and the civil authorities (Section 9.2.1), the major religious superior will meet the accused religious in person and inform him or her that an allegation has been received and that it is being dealt with in accordance with the Church's policies and procedures for the protection of children. The manner and timing by which the major religious superior is to inform the accused individual is to be guided by the conclusions of the meeting between the Director of Child Protection and the civil authorities, bearing in mind the rights in natural justice of the accused religious.

On communicating the allegation:

- The major religious superior will provide a summary of the substance of the allegation to the accused religious.

- The accused religious is to be reminded of his or her right not to respond to or admit to any offence, and of his or her right to legal representation and a canonical advisor.
- The major religious superior will ensure that the accused religious understands that anything they say may be introduced as evidence in a civil court or in the canonical process outlined in canon 695.
- The accused religious cannot be obliged to confess, sacramentally or non-sacramentally, to the allegation, nor should the major religious superior who is also a priest agree to hear the confession of an accused religious.
- The major religious superior will ask the accused religious to meet the Director of Child Protection to hear the details of the allegation as soon as he or she has chosen a legal and canonical advisor.
- The major religious superior is to provide a list of Support Persons who will be available to meet the accused religious to offer him or her pastoral support.
- The major religious superior will provide the accused religious with a list of canonical advisors, but will respect the right of the accused religious to choose a canonical advisor other than one of those listed.
- The major religious superior will explain that pastoral care will be offered to the family of the accused religious.

The major religious superior will communicate to the accused religious a Precept directing that he or she have no contact prior to the completion of an investigation with the person who has made the allegation, their family and/or the person who brought forward the allegation.

The major religious superior is to convene a meeting of his or her Child Protection Committee as soon as possible, to assist him or her in the ongoing response to the allegation.

10.3.3 Canonical investigation

The major religious superior is to collect the evidence concerning the facts and the imputability of the offence. The accusation and the evidence are then to be presented to the accused religious, who will be given an opportunity to present a defence. All the acts of evidence, signed by the major religious superior and the notary, are to be forwarded, together with the written and signed replies of the accused religious, to the superior general (canon 695, §2).[60]

10.3.4 Responsibilities of the Director of Child Protection

The Director of Child Protection will follow the same procedure as that outlined above for diocesan and religious clergy (Section 10.2.4).

10.3.5 Leave from ministry for religious who are not ordained

A religious against whom an allegation of child abuse has been made can be removed from ministry at the discretion of the authority which made the appointment, with prior notice being given to the religious superior, or by the religious superior, with prior notice being given to the appointing authority. Neither requires the other's consent (canon 682, §2). The rights of the accused religious remain intact.

At any point, an accused religious or member of a society of apostolic life is free to seek an indult of departure.

10.4 Procedures Relating to a Bishop or Religious Superior

When an allegation or suspicion of child abuse has been reported to the civil authorities about a bishop, the bishop himself must immediately inform the Holy See. If he fails to do so, the Metropolitan is to refer the matter at once to the Holy See;[61] if there is no Metropolitan, or if he is the person against whom an allegation or report of suspicion has been made, it is the Suffragan senior by promotion who is to refer the matter in a manner similar to that outlined in canon 415. In the case of a major religious superior, the matter must be referred immediately to the superior general.

10.5 Procedures where Child Abuse is Non-Sexual

When an accusation of non-sexual child abuse (that is, physical or emotional abuse or neglect) has been received and reported to the relevant civil authorities, the following are the procedures to be followed.

10.5.1 Diocesan cleric

The diocesan bishop will initiate an investigation and if, after consulting with the Child Protection Committee, he concludes that the ministry of the accused priest constitutes a risk to children and young people or is a cause of scandal to the faithful, he may limit the ministry of the accused cleric for the good of the Church (*pro bono Ecclesiae*) by appropriate disciplinary action, such as a singular Precept (canons 48–58).

If the facts demonstrate that the ministry of the priest has become harmful or at least ineffective, the diocesan bishop can, in accordance with canons 1740–1747, remove a parish priest from his parish or, in accordance with canon 552, remove a curate from office.

10.5.2 Religious

In the case of a religious or a member of a society of apostolic life, the religious superior is to collect the evidence and consult with his or her Council about how to proceed (canons 696–699).

11.1 Investigation Process

In the Republic of Ireland, allegations of child abuse are investigated by the Health Service Executive and by An Garda Síochána. These investigations may run concurrently or at different times.

In Northern Ireland, joint investigations and interviewing arrangements by the the Health and Social Services Trusts and the PSNI have been established under a joint protocol.[62]

11.1.1 Health services investigation

Investigations by the Health Service Executive or the Health and Social Services Trusts are undertaken to assess whether a child has been abused; they can lead to three possible outcomes:

- Confirmed   child abuse occurred.
- Inconclusive – unable to determine whether or not child abuse occurred.
- Confirmed non-abuse – child abuse did not occur.

11.1.2 Garda or PSNI investigation

Investigations by An Garda Síochána or the PSNI are undertaken to assess whether a criminal offence occurred. Following the investigation, the file is forwarded to the Director of Public Prosecutions.

If the Director of Public Prosecutions decides that the case should proceed to court, the outcome may be:

- conviction;
- acquittal;
- mis-trial – no determination of whether an offence occurred;
- *nolle prosequi* – where the prosecution withdraws the charge of an offence.

The Director of Public Prosecutions may, however, decide that the case should not proceed to court. This decision may indicate that the Director of Public Prosecutions considers that the evidence would not meet the standard of proof required by a criminal court, but it does not necessarily imply innocence.

11.2 Outcome of Investigation

11.2.1 Outcome unclear as to whether child abuse occurred

If the outcome of the investigations by the civil authorities is unclear as to whether child abuse did occur, the Professional Practice Committee of the National Board for Child Protection (see Chapter Two, Section 2.2.2) will assess the situation, having regard to the safety and protection of children and young people, and shall inform the bishop or religious superior or chairperson of the Church organisation of its assessment.

11.2.2 Finding that child abuse did occur

Where the determination is that child abuse did occur, and the person is a priest or religious, the procedures outlined in Chapter Twelve should be followed.

11.2.3 False or mistaken allegations

Few allegations of child abuse are deemed to be false; however, those that are unfounded cause profound distress to the people who are wrongly accused. Given the gravity of an accusation of child abuse, it is important that when an allegation is deemed to be false or mistaken, all appropriate steps are taken by the Church authorities to restore the good name of the priest, religious or lay person who has been wrongly accused. The bishop, religious superior or chairperson, in consultation with the person against whom the allegation was made, shall decide on how they are to be supported and facilitated in resuming their duties.

Depending on the particular circumstances of the person falsely accused, the steps that should be taken by the bishop, religious superior or chairperson to publicly restore the good name of the person could include:

- Issuing a press release and making a statement from the pulpit explaining that the allegation or allegations had been deemed to be false.
- The manager or chairperson of the relevant organisation or group making a statement to all staff and parent groups that the allegation or allegations had been deemed to be false.
- Appointing a mentor to support the person falsely accused, particularly in regard to their re-entry into ministry or employment.
- Publicly reinstating the exonerated person in the presence of the bishop or relevant religious superior.

In addition, a falsely accused person can institute a canonical and/or civil action against those who made the false allegation. In the Republic of Ireland, the Protections for Persons Reporting Child Abuse Act, 1998 (s. 5) provides that it is a criminal offence for a person to make a report of child abuse to the appropriate authorities 'knowing that statement to be false'.

In Northern Ireland, where an allegation is made in bad faith, the person wrongly accused can seek recourse under the laws of slander, libel or malicious prosecution.

12 Protecting Against Future Risk

12.1 Introduction

Taking just and appropriate action to protect against future risk is an essential element of an effective child protection policy in which the welfare of the child is paramount. This chapter outlines actions to be taken to protect against future risk once a priest or religious has been convicted of child abuse, or where such abuse has been admitted or established but there has not been a conviction.

12.2 Assessment and Treatment

The effective protection of children and the elimination of future risk require rigorous and professional assessment, treatment and ongoing management of those who have abused children or who are considered to pose a risk. Bishops and religious superiors require professional support and advice in meeting their complex responsibilities in this area. With the welfare of the child as the paramount consideration, the following procedures should be observed.

12.2.1 Assessment

Assessment is a complex and specialised process which should be carried out by an accredited multi-disciplinary team of clinicians, trained and experienced in assessing such cases. All priests and religious who have abused children or who are considered to pose a risk shall be requested to undergo such an assessment.

It is important that an agreement or contract is made between those who are carrying out the assessment and the person being assessed, whereby:

- a commitment is given that all relevant information will be made available to the assessment process;
- a commitment is given that those who carry out the assessment will make all reports available to the person assessed and to his or her bishop or religious superior.

12.2.2 Treatment

Where, as a result of assessment, a priest or religious is deemed to require professional treatment, such treatment should be provided. It is essential that all treatment programmes used by Church authorities are properly accredited. Advice on this matter will be available from the National Office for Child Protection.

In order to benefit from treatment, it is important that the person concerned acknowledges that he or she has committed an offence, recognises the harm done to the person (or persons) abused and shows a willingness to participate actively in treatment.

12.3 Future Status Regarding Ministry

Given that the abuse of children is a crime and a profound breach of the sacred trust vested in a priest or religious, the options for the future ministry of those who have abused are greatly diminished and, in some cases, removed altogether.

Where a priest or religious has been convicted of the criminal offence of the abuse of a child, that person shall not be allowed to return to any form of ministry which would permit any access to, or contact with, children or young people. (This is without prejudice to a person's right to appeal under canon law or civil law.)

Where child abuse has been admitted or it has been established that a priest or religious has abused a child or is a risk to children, but investigations by the civil authorities have not resulted in a conviction of child abuse, the bishop or religious superior is to initiate the appropriate process in canon law.

A suitably trained Support Person shall be appointed to provide ongoing pastoral support to a priest or religious convicted of child abuse, or about whom concerns exist.

12.3.1 Referral to Professional Practice Committee

In the process of considering the future of a priest or religious who has been the subject of concerns regarding child abuse, a bishop or religious superior will have available the expertise of the Professional Practice Committee (Chapter Two, Section 2.2.2).

Before referring a case to the Professional Practice Committee, however, the bishop or religious superior should be satisfied that the following conditions have been met:

- The priest or religious concerned has completed a comprehensive professional assessment and treatment programme.
- An appropriate period of time after treatment has passed, during which the behaviour of the priest or religious has been observed.
- An after-care programme, involving individual and group therapy,

has been put in place to provide continuing support and guidance to the priest or religious.

- The priest or religious has accepted that should there be any proposal to assign him or her to some form of limited ministry, it will be necessary to disclose his or her past abusing to those in authority in the proposed assignment and to such others as might need to know.
- A system of individual supervision and monitoring has been put in place to ensure accountability.

In making its determination, the Professional Practice Committee will satisfy itself that it has available to it all the relevant information and reports in relation to the priest or religious, as well as access to the necessary expertise in risk assessment.

The Professional Practice Committee will then advise on whether and in what circumstances, if at all, the person may ever again be permitted to resume some form of limited public ministry.

12.3.2 Future ministry not possible

If the Professional Practice Committee rules out appointment to any ministry, the options available are described below.

In the case of a diocesan priest these include:

- retirement under strictly monitored conditions;
- laicisation sought by the priest;
- the imposition of ecclesiastical penalties, not excluding, if the case so warrants, dismissal from the clerical state, in accordance with the processes prescribed in canon law.

In relation to a religious who has offended, an option may be that the person will live the religious life within their religious community, without being permitted access to children. This will require careful supervision of the person concerned and attention to the practical and pastoral needs of the religious community, as outlined in Section 12.4.3 below.

12.3.3 Limited assignment to ministry

If the Professional Practice Committee advises that a limited assignment to ministry is possible, the bishop or religious superior should make the assignment by way of a written Precept, which will include the following elements:

- a recommitment by the priest or religious to the way of life into which they have been ordained and/or professed;
- details of the place of residence of the priest or religious and the specific terms of their assignment;
- the conditions of supervision which will apply during the assignment;
- the requirement that the priest or religious will participate in an appropriate and specified programme of therapy;
- the requirement that the priest or religious will avoid being alone with children;
- the requirement that the priest or religious will abide by the Code of Behaviour for personnel which is operative in the position to which he or she is assigned;
- an acceptance that his or her past in relation to concerns about suitability for ministry with children will be disclosed to those in authority at the place of assignment and to such others as may need to know;
- a clear and unequivocal statement that violation of the requirements outlined in the Precept shall result in the person's immediate removal from the assignment.

12.4 Supervision

The supervision of those convicted of child abuse is a civil responsibility, but relevant religious authorities also have an important role in this area.

12.4.1 Formal notification of supervision

The bishop or religious superior shall advise the priest or religious in writing of the monitoring process which is to be put in place.

The priest or religious concerned shall acknowledge in writing acceptance and understanding of the monitoring process.

12.4.2 Supervision of the monitored priest or religious

Each priest or religious who is to be supervised should be assigned to a willing, competent priest or religious who has their confidence and that of the bishop or religious superior. This person should have an understanding of the nature of the abuse and have professional support.

It is important that the proposed supervision, living arrangements and meaningful activity or work are agreed with the priest or religious concerned in ways that maximise their cooperation and compliance.

12.4.3 Supervision within religious communities

Where the person to be supervised is to be part of a religious community, it is important that the other members of the community are given adequate advice and support in relation to their role, including information on the relevant clinical and practical issues involved. In particular:

- The community should discuss the matter in advance of the person concerned taking up residence. It may also be helpful to have a meeting in the presence of the person to be supervised, once they have arrived.
- Other members of the community may find the situation particularly stressful. It is important that they are provided with adequate support, including the assistance of qualified counsellors, if necessary.
- The person being supervised may also have difficulty integrating into the life of the religious community. They, too, should be provided with adequate support, including qualified counselling, if necessary.
- It is important that the person being supervised is encouraged to co-operate sensitively and constructively with the community as it seeks to support them in observing the agreed monitoring process.
- The person being supervised should meet regularly with the local superior and/or regional superior to review their life in the religious community.

13.1   Introduction

Throughout his ministry, Jesus reached out to those who were hurt or wounded in any way. The Church is called to continue this vital ministry of healing and reconciliation.

The principles and procedures outlined in this chapter seek to ensure that those affected by child abuse are supported on the journey towards healing and reconciliation through the provision of a comprehensive range of human, practical, professional and spiritual supports.

These supports are based on a recognition that the abuse or alleged abuse of a child or young person in the Church can have far-reaching and painful consequences not only for the child or young person themselves, but also for their family and their local community, as well as for the accused person's family, colleagues and community.

The supports are based also on an acknowledgement that an effective pastoral care response requires the involvement of those who have awareness of the short- and long-term effects of child abuse and sensitivity towards the needs of all of those concerned, as well as relevant professional expertise.

13.2   Victims of Abuse and their Families

13.2.1 Impact of abuse

The pastoral response to victims must take account of the profound effects of child abuse, the devastating impact it may have had on the life of the victim and the reality that, in some instances, he or she will have been living with the pain of their abuse for many years before reporting.

Furthermore, for most people, the process of disclosing abuse will be an emotionally distressing experience. In particular, the possibility that they will not be believed may cause anxiety. For this reason, it is important that assurance is given to those who have reported allegations in good faith that they have done the right thing in disclosing the abuse.

In some instances, people may experience feelings of anger and depression which can lead them to reject offers of pastoral help. However, it should be recognised that there may be other times when they will be more open to accepting pastoral support. Pastoral outreach should take cognisance of this: there must be respect for the wishes of those who do not want to avail of pastoral care when it is first offered, while at the same time ensuring that it can be accessed later, if so wished.

13.2.2 Pastoral care needs

The person who has been abused, or the families of children who have been abused, may have the following pastoral needs:

- to know that they are being listened to, believed and respected;
- to know that they are recognised as individuals with particular needs;
- to know that the suffering and the pain they have experienced prior to the time of the disclosure will be acknowledged;
- to be given information regarding the Church and civil processes which will follow;
- to be kept informed;
- to know whether the alleged offender has admitted or denied the allegation;
- to have access to support;
- to have access to professional counselling;
- to have spiritual guidance and help with the practice of their faith.

13.2.3 Recommended steps

- Following the reporting of an allegation of child abuse by the Director of Child Protection, the bishop or religious superior (or person so delegated) should communicate immediately with the alleged victim, acknowledging the allegation and offering them support.
- The bishop or religious superior should offer to meet the alleged victim or their family, if the victim is a minor.
- Where a victim does not want contact with the Church, this should be respected.
- If the alleged victim does wish to have contact, the Church will offer the services of a Support Person to the victim and their family. A choice of male or female, clerical or lay Support Person should be offered.
- The victim should be kept informed of developments as they unfold, including being told of the outcome of the meeting between the Director of Child Protection and the civil authorities (Chapter Nine, Section 9.2.1). Where the offer of a Support Person has been accepted, the Support Person will act as a liaison between the alleged victim and the Director of Child Protection.
- Spiritual help should to be offered to the victim. The person providing spiritual help and support must have a knowledge and appreciation of the dynamics and impact of child abuse. The spiritual advisor may be a priest, religious or lay person. The victim

should have the option of having an advisor from outside his or her local area.

- The victim of child abuse should have access to professional counselling, if they so wish. The Support Person should facilitate this through referral to an appropriate professional counsellor.
- In the case of an allegation being reported to the Church by a third party, pastoral support should be offered to the person alleging the abuse through that third party and not directly.
- Where possible, the victim should be informed of the response of the accused to the allegation, including whether they are admitting or denying the allegation.
- The Director of Child Protection should regularly review the support being provided to victims and their families by the relevant diocese or religious congregation.
- Where appropriate, the Support Person should be available to accompany the victim to criminal court proceedings.
- Where appropriate, and after a suitable period of time, a follow-up letter should be sent by the bishop or religious superior (or person so delegated) as a statement of continuing concern.

13.3   Local Church Communities

13.3.1 Impact of revelations of abuse

An allegation of abuse against a priest, religious, employee or volunteer will have a major impact on the parish, religious congregation, school or Church organisation concerned. Reactions may include anger, hurt, confusion or alienation from the Church.

Many parents will also have anxiety about any interactions their children may have had with the alleged offender. A lack of an immediate response in this situation and a failure to provide appropriate information can lead to the circulation of erroneous rumours which are not in the interests of the alleged victim(s) or the person accused. Addressing the particular needs of Church communities in which an allegation of child abuse has been made is, therefore, a vital and urgent part of an effective response.

13.3.2 Pastoral care needs

Whether an allegation concerns current, recent or historical abuse, the Church communities affected will need:

- appropriate and accurate information;
- assurance that the relevant civil authorities have been advised and that appropriate action is being taken;
- advice on child protection principles and procedures;
- spiritual support;
- emotional support, particularly for parents of other children in the community concerned.

13.3.3 Recommended steps

- The bishop or religious superior should respond promptly to the needs of the relevant community once an allegation has become public.
- Following an allegation, it may be appropriate for those with immediate responsibility for the pastoral care of the particular community to facilitate a 'community forum'. The purpose of such a forum will be to identify areas of specific support needed; to enable anxieties within the community to be expressed; and to begin to identify strategies to address damaged relationships within the Church community.
- When an allegation of child abuse has been received, the parish priest, or local religious superior, in any other place where the accused person held an appointment shall be informed.
- When an allegation has been proven, the bishop or religious superior will visit the community and publicly acknowledge the hurt caused to the victim (or victims), their family, the Church community and all those affected.
- The bishop or religious superior should be conscious that there may be other people within the community who have been abused but who have not yet approached the Church. Assurances should be given that should any such person wish to come forward their concerns will be listened to and dealt with sensitively and with compassion.
- Priests or religious appointed to a parish or community where there has been an allegation of child abuse should be given adequate preparation so that they can respond sensitively to the needs of the parish or local community. They should be assured that continuing support will be available to them.
- Consideration should be given to holding special liturgical services which reflect and respond to the needs of the parish or community. The timing and frequency of these services should be decided in consultation with representatives of the local community.

13.4   The Person Accused

A person who has been accused of child abuse will require emotional, spiritual and practical support. They may be subject to a range of feelings including fear, isolation, guilt, anger, depression and denial. They may have particular concerns in regard to practical issues such as future income and accommodation. For these reasons, it is important that the person accused receives reassurance that the necessary emotional, spiritual and legal supports will be provided in accordance with the procedures outlined in Chapters Nine and Ten. This includes the offer of a Support Person and access to professional counselling, if requested.

The procedure to be followed when a priest or religious, or lay church employee or volunteer has been found to be the subject of a false or mistaken allegation is outlined under 'False or mistaken allegations' in Chapter Eleven, Section 11.2.3.

13.5   Family of the Person Accused

13.5.1 Pastoral care needs

Once aware of the allegation, the accused person's family will have to cope with many conflicting emotions. They may feel isolated, ashamed, stigmatised, concerned for the well-being of the accused and unsure as to where to turn for help.

The family of the accused person may have the following pastoral care needs:

- to have their concerns and anxieties heard and acknowledged;
- to know that their family member will be treated in a fair and just manner;
- to know how the civil and Church processes involved will proceed;
- to be kept informed on a regular basis;
- to have practical advice and support;
- to have advice on how to respond to the media, should the situation arise;
- to have spiritual guidance and support.

13.5.2 Recommended steps

- If the alleged offender has given permission, the bishop or religious superior should write to the family of the alleged offender acknowledging the distress that arises following an allegation, offering support and indicating a willingness to meet with them should they so wish.

- A follow-up letter should be sent as a statement of continuing interest.
- The Church should indicate that a Support Person will be provided for family members, should they so wish.
- Advice should be given on how to respond to any media queries.
- Family members may wish to have the support of professional counselling; the Support Person should facilitate them in accessing this.

13.6 Colleagues of the Person Accused

13.6.1 Impact of allegation of abuse

The colleagues of an accused person in a parish or religious congregation may experience a range of emotions when they learn that an allegation of child abuse has been made. They may feel anxiety about the welfare of both the alleged victim and the accused, about the impact of the allegation on the parish or religious community, about the practical implications for the administration of the parish or the work of the religious community and about the impact of such an allegation on their own reputation and identity. Their anxieties and concerns, may, in turn, lead to a general loss of morale.

13.6.2 Pastoral care needs

Colleagues of an accused person will have the following specific needs:

- to be given initial information and to be kept informed about all relevant aspects of the process as it unfolds, where legally appropriate;
- to know that the practical and emotional impact on them of the allegation is recognised, including the possible increase in workload that may arise as a result of the accused person taking administrative leave;
- to be assured that the process for dealing with the allegation against their colleague will be fair and just;
- to be advised on how to respond sensitively and adequately to all those immediately affected, including parishioners;
- to have advice on how to deal with media queries;
- to have ongoing practical and emotional support from their leaders.

13.6.3 Recommended steps

- The bishop or religious superior will appoint an appropriate person to meet the colleagues of an accused person as soon as possible after an allegation has been reported. Arrangements for the ongoing support of colleagues should be discussed and agreed at this meeting. The alleged offender should be informed that this process has taken place.
- Colleagues should be given advice and support on how to respond in a sensitive, honest and non-defensive way when the allegation becomes public.
- A meeting should also be arranged with the accused person's former colleagues in places where he or she previously ministered, was employed or worked as a volunteer.

APPENDICES

Appendix One
Working Group on Child Protection

Ms Maureen Lynott (Chairperson)
Mr Paul Bailey, Director of Child Protection Office, Irish Bishops'
Conference
Sr Martina Barrett, CORI Child Protection Task Force
Ms Margaret Burns, former Administrator, Council for Social Welfare
Ms Marie Collins, Survivor of Clerical Child Sexual Abuse
Fr Hugh Connolly, Lecturer in Theology, St Patrick's College, Maynooth
Monsignor John Crowley, Representative of the National Conference of
Priests in Ireland
Sr Evelyn Greene, CORI Child Protection Task Force – Education
Ms Kay Hyden, National Co-ordinator of Training and Development, Child
Protection Office, Irish Bishops' Conference
Dr Kevin McCoy, Consultant, Social Care Services
Fr Michael Mullaney, Lecturer in Canon Law
Fr Paul Murphy, Director CORI Child Protection Office
Ms Marguerite O'Neill, Senior Clinical Psychologist
Mr Patrick O'Toole, Retired Assistant Garda Commissioner
Ms Suzanne Phelan, Background in child protection and social work
Ms Gemma Rowley, Social Worker; Representative of Bishops' Committee
on Child Protection
Fr David Smith, CORI Child Protection Task Force
Mr Michael Waters, Chairperson, Survivors of Child Abuse (UK)

Ms Liz Chaloner (Drafter)
Mr Ger Crowley (Special Advisor)

Administrative Support
Ms Andrea Horan, Child Protection Office, Irish Bishops' Conference
Ms Colma McEvoy, Child Protection Office, Irish Bishops' Conference

Appendix Two

Written Submissions to the Working Group on Child Protection: Main Points

- There was wide agreement that the Catholic Church should be an example of best practice in the prevention of child abuse and that its new policies and procedures on child protection should be fully consistent with civil law and guidance. These policies and procedures should be implemented uniformly across all Church bodies and by all those working for the Church, in whatever capacity. As a general principle, it was agreed that the safety and welfare of the child should be paramount.

- The importance of transparent auditing and monitoring procedures was emphasised, as was the need for resources for implementation, systematic training and awareness-raising for all those whose work brings them into regular contact with children.

- There was a specific recommendation that there should be a child-friendly version of the Church's new child protection policies. This should include a complaints procedure that would be accessible to children.

- Concern was expressed that all those working with children in the Church should gain police clearance in advance of taking up positions, whether paid or voluntary.

- With regard to the determination of suitability of candidates for the priesthood, it was recommended that a single national database be established and maintained by the Church which would hold information on all applicants for ordained ministry and be available to selection boards, bishops and religious superiors.

- There should be strict adherence to the Instruction of the Holy See and *Decreta Generalia* of the Irish Bishops' Conference on admitting candidates coming from other seminaries or religious houses.

- The challenge of reconciling canon law and civil law was highlighted in several submissions.

- It was pointed out that where there is a lack of pastoral or therapeutic response from either the Church or State to child abuse, the person abused is left isolated and with little alternative but to seek redress through the courts.

- The rights of the accused were raised in a number of submissions. It was emphasised that the person accused has Constitutional rights which need to be safeguarded, while the welfare and protection of children must also be ensured.

- There were differing opinions regarding the placing of those accused on 'administrative leave'. On the one hand, it was recommended that accused persons should be removed from duty, not as a presumption of guilt but as a necessary precaution. On the other hand, major concerns were expressed about the accused being asked to take administrative leave without an investigation being completed.
- Fears were expressed about the possibility of false allegations. The difficulty of restoring the good name of a person who has been falsely accused was stressed.
- Attention was drawn to the need for more expeditious investigations into allegations of child abuse. There was a suggestion that levels of communication between the Church and civil authorities needed to be improved.
- The point was made that lack of a criminal conviction does not necessarily imply innocence, especially in light of the very low rate of prosecution in the criminal courts and the even lower rate of conviction.
- Many submissions expressed concerns about sex education programmes in Catholic schools. Some suggested that these should be withdrawn from the curriculum; others argued that sex education was a central element of a child protection policy.
- A number of submissions sought clarity in reporting procedures.
- It was suggested that clear guidelines were required in relation to allegations of child abuse made against bishops, religious superiors, delegates and others in positions of authority in the Church.

Appendix Three

Key Legislative Provisions

Republic of Ireland
The Child Care Act, 1991
Domestic Violence Act, 1996
The Non-Fatal Offences Against the Person Act, 1997
Freedom of Information Act, 1997
Protections for Persons Reporting Child Abuse Act, 1998
Data Protection Act, 1988 and the Data Protection (Amendment) Act, 2003
The Education Act, 1998
Education (Welfare) Act, 2000
Health Act, 2004

Northern Ireland
The Children (Northern Ireland) Order 1995
The Children's Evidence (Northern Ireland) Order 1995
Data Protection Act 1998
Family Homes and Domestic Violence (Northern Ireland) Order 1998
Human Rights Act 1998
The Public Interest Disclosure Order 1998

Appendix Four

Recommended Supervision Ratios

In the Republic of Ireland, the Childcare (Pre-School Services) Regulations, 1996 and Child Care (Pre-School Services) (Amendment) Regulations, 1997 have the following requirements for adult:child ratios:[63]

Service	Age	Adult:Child Ratio
Full Day Care	0–1 year	1:3
	1–3 years	1:6
	3–6 years	1:8
Sessional	0–6 years	1:10
Drop-in Centre	1–6 years	1:8
	under 12 months	1:3

The *Code of Practice – Child Protection for the Youth Work Sector* recommends the following:

> The minimum adult: young person ratio should ideally be **one adult per group of eight plus one other adult, and allowing an additional adult for each group of eight thereafter**. Local circumstances, the ages of the children, the experience of the volunteers and the staff should be taken into consideration. Safety, ability/disability of young people and the nature of the activities being undertaken may require that these ratios be considerably lower.[64]

In Northern Ireland, *Our Duty to Care: Principles of Good Practice for the Protection of Children and Young People* recommends the following ratios:

Age	Staff:Child Ratio
0–2 years	1 member of staff to 3 children
2–3 years	1 member of staff to 4 children
3–7 years	1 member of staff to 8 children
8 years and over	2 members of staff (preferably one of each gender) for up to 20 children

There should be one additional staff member for every ten extra children. The ratio of staff and volunteers to children with disabilities is dependent on the needs of the individual child.[65]

Appendix Five

Sample Application Form for Volunteers*
Confidential

Surname   --

Forename   --

Address   --

Date of Birth ---------------------------- Tel. --

Are you *(Please tick)*

Employed   -------------- Unemployed ---------------- Student -------------------

Homemaker -------------- Retired   ---------------- Other   -------------------

Previous work experience:

Have you previously been involved in voluntary work?   Yes ------ No ------

If yes, give details:

How much time can you commit to voluntary work? *(Please tick)*

	Mon	Tues	Wed	Thur	Fri	Sat	Sun
Morning							
Afternoon							
Evening							

* From: Department of Health and Children, *Our Duty to Care: the Principles of Good Practice for the Protection of Children and Young People*, Dublin: Stationery Office, 2001, pp 41–2.

Do you have any spare time hobbies, interests or activities?

Any other relevant information?

Please provide the names and addresses of two people whom we could contact for a reference (not relatives)

Name	----------------------	Name	----------------------
Address	----------------------	Address	----------------------
	----------------------		----------------------
	----------------------		----------------------
	----------------------		----------------------
Tel.	----------------------	Tel.	----------------------

Signed ---------------------- Date ----------------------

Other information which might be sought on the application form
- Can you drive? Do you have access to a car?
- How did you learn about this volunteering opportunity?
- Why do you want to do voluntary work?
- Have you any disability which would affect your voluntary work?
- Have you ever committed a criminal offence?

Appendix Six

Sample Declaration Form to be Completed by Staff and Volunteers*
Confidential

Declaration from all staff and volunteers working with children and young people

Surname   ---
Forename   ---
Address   ---
Tel.   ---
Date of Birth -------------------------- Place of Birth ------------------------------------

Any other name previously known as --

Do you have any prosecutions pending or have you ever been convicted of a criminal offence or been the subject of a caution or of a bind over order?

Yes ---------- No ----------

If yes, please state below the nature and date(s) of the offence(s), the court responsible for dealing with the matter, the approximate date of the court hearing.

Nature of offence -------------------------- Date of offence ----------------------------
                   --------------------------   ----------------------------
                   --------------------------   ----------------------------
                   --------------------------   ----------------------------
                   --------------------------   ----------------------------

Signed -- Date --

---

*   Adapted from: *Our Duty to Care: Principles of Good Practice for the Protection of Children and Young People*, Information Pack, Belfast: Volunteer Development Agency, 2000.

Appendix Seven

Pre-Employment Consultancy Service (Northern Ireland)

Organisations or groups wishing to use this service need to make an application to the Child Care Unit of the Department of Health, Social Services and Public Safety (see details below). The Pre-Employment Consultancy Service (PECS) can be used by those organisations which clearly meet the criterion of having posts involving 'substantial access' to children or to adults with a learning disability.

In applying to use the service the following information must be included:

- A description of the organisation
- Details of the organisation: its structure and constitution, the names and addresses of all office bearers (chairperson, treasurer, secretary, committee members)
- Details of the posts which involve 'substantial access' to children (or adults with a learning disability), including the nature of the access, and the reasons why such access cannot be avoided
- Written confirmation that the organisation will conform as far as possible to the principles outlined in *Our Duty to Care: Principles of Good Practice for the Protection of Children and Young People.*

For further information contact:

Pre-Employment Consultancy Service
Child Care Unit
Department of Health, Social Services and Public Safety
Room 508a Dundonald House
Upper Newtownards Road
Belfast BT4
Tel 028-9052 2559
Email: pecs@dhsspsni.gov.uk

Further information about the service is contained in the Department of Health, Social Services and Public Policy booklet, *Safer Organisations: Safer Children*, which is also available from the Child Care Unit.

Appendix Eight*

Sample Questionnaire for the Bishop or Religious Superior of a Priest or Religious Applying for Transfer

Name of applying priest or religious

Name of his Diocese or Religious Congregation

----

1. Why does the applying priest or religious want to minister in the Diocese of ---?

2. Does he seek ministry in the Diocese of -- with a view to permanence and/or incardination?

                                                    Yes ------------ No --------

3. Is he coming temporarily?

                                                    Yes ------------ No ------------

4. If he is a member of an Institute of Consecrated Life or Apostolic Life, is he currently Exclaustrated?

                                                    Yes ------------ No ------------

5. Has he ever petitioned the Holy See for secularisation *praevio experimento* in accord with canon 693? If yes, give details.

                                                    Yes ------------ No ------------

----

----

6. Have you any specific concerns about the performance of his ministry? If yes, give details.

                                                    Yes ------------ No ------------

----

----

7. Have there ever been accusations or charges against him for sexual misconduct? If yes, give details.

                                                    Yes ------------ No ------------

----

----

8. Have there ever been accusations against him concerning any form of impropriety towards children or young people? If yes, give details.

                                                    Yes ------------ No ------------

----

----

9. Has he ever shown any behaviour that would indicate that he is a risk to children or young people? If yes, give details.

Yes ----------- No -----------

----

10. Has he ever been arrested or had a criminal charge made against him? If yes, give details.

Yes ----------- No -----------

----

11. Are there any other reasons why you would not recommend him for ministry in this diocese, or accept him back into your own diocese for pastoral ministry? If yes, please give reasons.

Yes ----------- No -----------

----

12. Any additional comments

I testify that the above-named priest, who is applying for ministry in the Diocese of --

is a priest in good standing in his Diocese / Religious Congregation and has my permission to seek to exercise priestly ministry in the Diocese of

----

Name (please print) ------------------------- Title ----------------------------------
Signature ------------------------- Date ----------------------------------

Diocesan Seal

Statement Concerning a Priest Transferring to another Diocese

This is to state that   ---
is a priest in good standing in (name of Diocese or Religious Congregation)

- To the best of my knowledge in the external forum, I am of the opinion that he is of good character and reputation.
- I believe that he is qualified to perform his ministerial duties in an effective and suitable manner.
- I am unaware of anything in his background which would render him unsuitable to work with children or young people under the age of eighteen years.
- To the best of my knowledge, no accusations of sexual misconduct or sexual impropriety have ever been made against him; no criminal charge has ever been made against him, and he has never been suspended or otherwise canonically disciplined.
- I have no knowledge that he has a current untreated alcohol or substance abuse problem.

Therefore, I present -- (name of priest)
for faculties and/or appointment in the Diocese of

Name (please print)   ---- -------------------- Title ---------------------------------------
Signature   --------------------------- Date ---------------------------------------

Diocesan Seal

Appendix Nine

Clearance for a Member of a Religious Congregation Transferring to Ireland

When a member of a religious congregation is transferring to Ireland they are advised to bring two letters with them, one being a Letter of Clearance from their religious leader or major superior and the other a letter from their previous employer or from someone who has had first-hand knowledge of their previous work with children and young people.

The Letter of Clearance needs to contain the following information:

• Name of the person giving the Letter of Clearance;
• Position/occupation of that person;
• Name of the religious concerned;
• Length of time they have known the person concerned and in what capacity.

In addition, the Letter of Clearance should contain a response to the following question:

Is there any reason why the above-named person should not be given a position which involves working with children and young people? If so, please give details:

Signed -------------------------------------- Date ---

Appendix Ten

Role of State Agencies

Central Government

Central Government has the overall responsibility for safeguarding children and young people. It provides the legislative and structural framework through which services for the care and protection of children can be delivered. It provides national policies and guidelines, sets objectives and standards, monitors and reviews the delivery of services and has the responsibility of ensuring that the necessary resources are in place to achieve the targets set.

The statutory agencies with specific responsibilities for child protection and for investigating allegations and suspicions of child abuse are the Health Service Executive in the Republic of Ireland; the Health and Social Services Boards and Health and Social Services Trusts in Northern Ireland, and the police – An Garda Síochána and the PSNI.

Health Service Executive

In the Republic of Ireland, the Health Service Executive (HSE), established under the Health Act, 2004, took over the functions previously carried out by the health boards. The HSE has a range of statutory responsibilities in the area of child welfare, family support, child protection and child care arising from the provisions of the Child Care Act, 1991. The HSE is responsible for delivering services to children and young people in line with national objectives and standards. It has a statutory responsibility to assess child abuse cases from a child protection and welfare perspective and to take appropriate action to promote the welfare of the child.

Health and Social Services Boards and Health and Social Services Trusts

In Northern Ireland, Health and Social Services Boards (HSS Boards), in consultation with other agencies, have the duty to assess the requirements of, and plan services for, children in need in their area. They have the lead responsibility for the establishment and effective functioning of Area Child Protection Committees – the multi-agency committees which act as a focal point for local co-operation to safeguard children considered to be at risk of significant harm.

The Health and Social Services Trusts (HSS Trusts) have a statutory responsibility to investigate child abuse from a child protection and welfare perspective.

The respective duties of HSS Boards and the HSS Trusts are set out in the Children (NI) Order 1995.

Police Authorities

The involvement of An Garda Síochána and the PSNI in child abuse cases stems from their responsibilities to protect the community and bring offenders to justice. Where it is suspected that a crime has been committed, the police authorities will have overall responsibility for the direction of any criminal investigation. It is the function of the police authorities to interview and take statements which will form part of the criminal investigation file.

Although it is the task of the police authorities to investigate a possible crime, it is the Director of Public Prosecutions who has the ultimate responsibility for deciding whether a case will be prosecuted through the criminal courts.

Criminal courts require proof beyond reasonable doubt that the defendant committed the crime. The burden of proof rests with the prosecution to establish guilt to this standard of evidence. Where the Director of Public Prosecutions decides that a case should not proceed to court, this may be because it has been decided that the evidence available would not meet the standard of proof required by a criminal court; a decision not to prosecute does not necessarily imply that the accused person is innocent.

Appendix Eleven

Signs and Symptoms of Child Abuse*

1. **Signs and Symptoms of Child Neglect**
    - Abandonment or desertion.
    - Children persistently left alone without adequate care and supervision.
    - Malnourishment, lacking food, inappropriate food or erratic feeding.
    - Lack of warmth.
    - Lack of adequate clothing.
    - Lack of protection and exposure to danger, including moral danger, or lack of supervision appropriate to the child's age.
    - Persistent failure to attend school.
    - Non-organic failure to thrive, that is, a child not gaining weight, not alone due to malnutrition but also due to emotional deprivation.
    - Failure to provide adequate care for a child's medical problems.
    - Exploited, overworked.

2. **Signs and Symptoms of Emotional Child Abuse**
    - Rejection.
    - Lack of praise and encouragement.
    - Lack of comfort and love.
    - Lack of attachment.
    - Lack of proper stimulation (for example, fun and play).
    - Lack of continuity of care (for example, frequent moves).
    - Serious over-protectiveness.
    - Inappropriate non-physical punishment (for example, locking in bedrooms).
    - Family conflicts and/or violence.
    - Inappropriate expectations of a child's behaviour – relative to his or her age and stage of development.
    - Every child who is abused sexually or physically or who is neglected is also emotionally abused.

* Adapted from *Children First, National Guidelines for the Protection and Welfare of Children*, Dublin: Stationery Office, 1999, pp. 125–131.

3.   **Signs and Symptoms of Physical Abuse**
- Bruises.
- Fractures.
- Swollen joints.
- Burns or scalds.
- Abrasions or lacerations.
- Haemorrhages (retinal, subdural).
- Damage to body organs.
- Poisonings – repeated (by, for example, prescribed drugs or alcohol).
- Failure to thrive.
- Coma or unconsciousness.
- Death.

4.   **Signs and Symptoms of Child Sexual Abuse**

Non-contact sexual abuse
- Offensive sexual remarks, including statements the offender makes with regard to the child's sexual attributes, what he or she would like to do to the child and other sexual comments.
- Obscene phone calls.
- Independent 'exposure' involving the offender showing the victim his or her private parts and/or masturbating in front of the victim.
- 'Voyeurism' involving instances when the offender observes the victim in a state of undress or in activities that provide the offender with sexual gratification. These may include activities that others do not regard as even remotely sexually stimulating.

Sexual contact
- Any touching of the intimate body parts. The offender may fondle or masturbate the victim and/or get the victim to fondle and/or masturbate them. Fondling can be either outside or inside clothes. Also includes 'frottage', that is where the offender gains sexual gratification from rubbing his or her genitals against the victim's body or clothing.

Oral-genital sexual abuse
- Involves the offender licking, kissing, sucking or biting on the child's genitals or inducing the child to do the same to them.

Interfemoral sexual abuse
- Sometimes referred to as 'dry sex' or 'vulvar intercourse', involves the offender placing his penis between the child's thighs.

Penetrative sexual abuse

- 'Digital penetration' involving putting fingers in the vagina or anus, or both. Usually the victim is penetrated by the offender, but sometimes the offender gets the child to penetrate them.
- 'Penetration with objects' involving penetration of the vagina, anus or occasionally mouth with an object.
- 'Genital penetration' involving the penis entering the vagina, sometimes partially.
- 'Anal penetration' involving the penis penetrating the anus.

Sexual exploitation

- Involves situations of sexual victimisation where the person who is responsible for the exploitation may not have direct sexual contact with the child. Two types of this abuse are child pornography and child prostitution.
- 'Child pornography' includes still photography, videos and movies and, more recently, computer-generated pornography.
- 'Child prostitution' for the most part involves children of latency age or in adolescence. However, children as young as four and five are known to be abused in this way

Sexual abuse in combination with other abuse

- The sexual abuses described above may be found in combination with other abuses, such as physical abuse and urination and defecation on the victim. In some cases, physical abuse is an integral part of the sexual abuse; in others, drugs and alcohol may be given to the victim.

Carers and professionals should be alert to the following physical and behavioural signs that may indicate sexual abuse:

- Bleeding from the vagina or anus.
- Difficulty or pain in passing urine or faeces.
- An infection may occur secondary to sexual abuse, which may or may not be a definitive sexually transmitted disease. Professionals should be informed if a child has a persistent vaginal discharge or has warts or a rash in the genital area.
- Noticeable and uncharacteristic change of behaviour.
- Hints about sexual activity.
- Age-inappropriate understanding of sexual behaviour.
- Inappropriate seductive behaviour.
- Sexually aggressive behaviour with others.

- Uncharacteristic sexual play with peers or with toys.
- Unusual reluctance to join in normal activities which involve undressing, for example, games or swimming.

Particular behavioural signs and emotional problems suggestive of child abuse in young children (0–10):

- Mood change, for example acting out or the child becomes fearful or withdrawn.
- Lack of concentration (change in school performance).
- Bed wetting, soiling.
- Psychosomatic complaints: pains, headaches.
- Skin disorders.
- Nightmares, changes in sleep patterns.
- School refusal.
- Separation anxiety.
- Loss of appetite.
- Isolation.

Particular behavioural signs and emotional problems suggestive of child abuse in older children (over 10):

- Mood change, for example, depression, failure to communicate.
- Running away.
- Drug, alcohol, or solvent abuse.
- Self-mutilation.
- Suicide attempts.
- Delinquency.
- Truancy.
- Eating disorders.
- Isolation.

Endnotes

1. *Child Sexual Abuse: Framework for a Church Response – Report of the Irish Catholic Bishops' Advisory Committee on Child Sexual Abuse by Priests and Religious*, Dublin: Veritas, 1996.

2. In the Republic of Ireland, the following are the key documents: Department of Health and Children, *Children First: National Guidelines for the Protection and Welfare of Children*, Dublin: Stationery Office, 1999; Department of Health and Children, *Our Duty to Care: the Principles of Good Practice for the Protection of Children and Young People*, Dublin: Stationery Office, 2001; Department of Education and Science, *Child Protection: Guidelines and Procedures*, Dublin: Department of Education and Science, 2002; Department of Education and Science, *Code of Good Practice – Child Protection for the Youth Work Sector*, 2nd edition, Dublin: Stationery Office, 2003. In Northern Ireland, the key guidelines are: *Our Duty to Care: Principles of Good Practice for the Protection of Children and Young People*, 3rd edition, Belfast: Volunteer Development Unit, 2000; Department of Health, Social Services and Public Safety, *Co-operating to Safeguard Children*, Belfast: Department of Health, Social Services and Public Safety, 2003.

3. Helen Goode, Hannah McGee and Ciarán O'Boyle, *Time to Listen: Confronting Child Sexual Abuse by Catholic Clergy in Ireland*, Dublin: Liffey Press, 2003.

4. See Appendix One for membership of the Working Group.

5. Appendix Two summarises the main points made in these submissions.

6. Based on *Pacem in Terris* (Peace on Earth), 1963, various, in Austin Flannery OP, general editor, *Vatican Council II: Conciliar and Post-Conciliar Documents*, Dublin: Dominican Publications, 1998.

7. These principles are, for the most part, variously based upon and derived from the following documents of the Church: *Gaudium et Spes* (Pastoral Constitution on the Church in the Modern World) 1963; *Pacem in Terris* (Peace on Earth), 1963; *Decree on the Apostolate of Lay People*, 1965; *Declaration on Christian Education*, 1965, all available in Austin Flannery OP, general editor, *Vatican Council II: Conciliar and Post-Conciliar Documents*, Dublin: Dominican Publications, 1998; Pope John Paul II, *Familiaris Consortio: Apostolic Exhortation Regarding the Role of the Christian Family in the Modern World*, 22 November 1981, London: Catholic Truth Society; Pontifical Council for the Family, *Children: Springtime of the Family and Society*, Vatican, 11–13 October 2000; *Catechism of the Catholic Church*, Dublin: Veritas, 1994.

8. See Article 3; Article 34; Article 36; Article 39. The text of the UN Convention on the Rights of the Child can be found in *The National Children's Strategy, Our Children: Their Lives*, Dublin: Stationery Office, 2000, Appendix D, pp. 112–129. (Available www.nco.ie)

9. Note 2 details the publications containing these guidelines. Appendix Three lists child welfare legislation in both jurisdictions and other relevant legal provisions.

10. *Co-operating to Safeguard Children*, p. 11. The principle of the paramountcy of the welfare of the child is also reflected in various international and national legal instruments, including the UN Convention on the Rights of the Child, the Child Care Act, 1991 (Republic of Ireland) and the Children (Northern Ireland) Order 1995. For example, Section 3.2 (b) 1 of the Child Care Act 1991 states that those in positions of responsibility will 'regard the welfare of the child as the first and paramount consideration'.

11. For instance, hospitals, seminaries and houses of formation.

12. Some of the material in Section 3.2 is based on *Working with Children and Young People in the Catholic Church Community in Ireland: Good Practice and Guidelines*, July 2003, www.cpo.ie

13. The requirements of the data protection legislation of the relevant jurisdiction must be adhered to in retaining records – in the Republic of Ireland, the Data Protection Act, 1998 and the Data Protection (Amendment) Act, 2003 and in Northern Ireland, the Data Protection Act 1998. For further information, see www.dataprotection.ie and www.informationcommissioner.gov.uk

14. Department of Health and Children, *Our Duty to Care*, p. 8.

15. See sample Application Form for Volunteers, Appendix Five.

16. See sample Declaration Form to be Completed by Staff and Volunteers, Appendix Six.

17. Contact details: Garda Central Vetting Unit, Racecourse Road, Thurles, Co Tipperary, Tel: 0504 27300.

18. For further information on the Pre-Employment Consultancy Service (Northern Ireland), see Appendix Seven.

19. J. Clarke, *A Guide to Good Employment Practice in the Community and Voluntary Sector*, Dublin: Combat Poverty Agency, 2002, p. 15, par. 1.12.

20. For further information, see J. Clarke, *A Guide to Good Employment Practice in the Community and Voluntary Sector.*

21. Many of the principles included in this section are contained in *Child Sexual Abuse: Framework for a Church Response.*

22. Vatican II, *Gaudium et Spes* (Pastoral Constitution on the Church in the Modern World) (1963); *Decree on the Up to Date Renewal of Religious Life,*

1965; *Decree on the Training of Priests*, all in Austin Flannery OP, general editor, *Vatican Council II: Conciliar and Post-Conciliar Documents*, Dublin: Dominican Publications, 1998; Pope John Paul II, *Pastores Dabo Vobis: Apostolic Exhortation on the Formation of Priests in the Circumstances of the Present Day*, London: Catholic Truth Society, 1992; Congregation for Institutes of Consecrated Life and Societies of Apostolic Life, *Directives on Formation in Religious Institutes*, Rome: Vatican Polyglot Press 1990.

23. *Children First*, p. 38, ss 4.3.2; see also *Our Duty to Care: Principles of Good Practice for the Protection of Children and Young People*, Belfast: Volunteer Development Unit, 2000, pp. 22–3.
24. Department of Education Northern Ireland, *Pastoral Care in Schools: Child Protection*, Bangor, Co Down: Department of Education Northern Ireland, 1999, p. 11.
25. *Children First*, p. 41, ss 5.2.1.
26. *Children First*, p. 41, ss 5.2.2.
27. *Children First*, p. 41, ss 5.2.4.
28. In the relevant laws in both jurisdictions 'a child' means a person under the age of eighteen years. However, it excludes a person under eighteen who is or has been married.
29. *Co-operating to Safeguard Children*, p. 13.
30. *Children First*, p. 31, ss 3.2.1.
31. *Children First*, p. 31, ss 3.2.3.
32. *Co-operating to Safeguard Children*, p. 13.
33. *Children First*, p. 31, ss 3.2.3.
34. *Co-operating to Safeguard Children*, p. 13.
35. *Children First*, p. 31, ss 3.3.1.
36. *Children First*, p. 32, s. 3.4.
37. *Children First*, p. 33, ss 3.5.1. See also Sexual Offences (Amendment) Act, 2000, s. 3, hmso.gov.uk/acts/acts 2000
38. See *Towards Healing: Principles and Procedures in Responding to Complaints of Abuse against Personnel of the Catholic Church in Australia*, December 2000.
39. *Children First*, p. 86, ss 9.4.4.
40. *Children First*, p. 33, ss 3.6.1.
41. For more detailed information on peer sexual abuse, see *Co-operating to Safeguard Children*, pp. 68–72.
42. *Children First*, p. 40, ss 4.7.2.
43. Department of Health and Children, *Our Duty to Care*, p. 20.
44. *Children First*, p. 38, ss 4.3.1, 4.3.2
45. *Children First*, p. 38, ss 4.3.3.
46. *Children First*, p. 111; Department of Health and Children, *Our Duty to Care*, p. 21 and p. 25; *Our Duty to Care* (Northern Ireland Guidelines), p. 24.

47. *Children First*, p. 50, ss 6.7.4; Department of Health and Children, *Our Duty to Care*, p. 20; *Our Duty to Care* (Northern Ireland Guidelines), p. 24.
48. *Children First*, pp. 39–40, ss 4.6.1.
49. See, for example, Child Protection Task Force, Conference of Religious of Ireland, *Ministry with Integrity: A Consultation Document about Standards in Pastoral Ministry*, Dublin, 2001.
50. Ibid., Appendix 3, p. 23.
51. *Children First*, pp. 37–8, ss 4.3.1.
52. *Co-operating to Safeguard Children*, p. 45, s. 5.11.
53. *Children First*, p. 109, ss 12.2.1.
54. *Children First*, p. 111, ss 12.5.1 (iii).
55. For the purpose of this document, 'lay religious' are those referred to in canon 207, §2.
56. Canon 223, §2.
57. The term Ordinary means diocesan bishop, superiors of clerical religious institutes of pontifical rite and clerical societies of apostolic life (canon 134, §1).
58. Canon 49.
59. Major religious superiors mean those who govern an entire institute, or a province, or a part equivalent to a province, or an autonomous house. To these are added the abbot primate and the superior of a monastic congregation (canon 620).
60. The superior general means the superior who has authority over all provinces, houses and members of the institute, to be exercised in accordance with the institute's own law.
61. Canon 436.
62. 'Protocol for the Joint Investigation, by Social Workers and Police Officers, of Alleged and Suspected Child Abuse': see *Co-operating to Safeguard Children*, p. 28, s. 3.59.
63. Department of Health and Children, *Child Care (Pre-School Services) Regulations, 1996 and Child Care (Pre-School Services)(Amendment) Regulations, 1997* and *Explanatory Guide to Requirements and Procedures for Notification and Inspection*, Dublin: Stationery Office 1998, pp. 32–3.
64. Department of Education and Science, *Code of Good Practice – Child Protection for the Youth Work Sector*, 2nd edition, Dublin: Stationery Office, 2003, p. 13.
65. *Our Duty to Care: Principles of Good Practice for the Protection of Children and Young People*, Information Pack, Belfast: Volunteer Development Agency 2000, Action Checklist 6.